ORRID TALES OF
TECHNOLOGY

TELFORD TANAGER

Kendall Hunt
publishing company

www.kendallhunt.com
Send all inquiries to:
4050 Westmark Drive
Dubuque, IA 52004-1840

First and most importantly, to my sweet Skwoozn, who not only supported me in this effort, but encouraged me, was my cheering section, and my first, best critic. I also want to thank my family for understanding when I spent all that time in my office muttering at the Mac, and for graciously putting up with lectures over the things I learned (eye rolls and all!). And to Max, editor extraordinaire, who made my ramblings readable. Finally, I want to thank all the students who have found this material interesting and possibly valuable, it's for you, the students, that I write this.

With love an appreciation,
Telford

CONTENTS

PREFACE

INTRODUCTION

So why do you have to have another book? I mean, don't you have more than enough books already? Well, because this is the only way I know of to give you some information that I feel is terribly critical to your understanding of this crazy, sometimes dangerous, digital world that is rapidly changing the way we communicate, do business, travel, and live. I've taught computer science for over 20 years now, and I have played with these amazing, frustrating, and sometimes frightening machines since the early 1970s. I have witnessed many changes, the most significant being how these devices have become so intertwined into our daily lives. Most of us are more or less dependent on our digital companions; my iPad goes everywhere with me!

So why this book? Well, because this book covers subjects that, while critical, either aren't addressed or are barely touched upon in the standard "Introduction to Computers" textbooks. Subjects that aren't historically part of the introductory curriculum. While the world of technology has rapidly evolved, our way of introducing students to the subject still focuses on the internals of the machine, and on learning one of the productivity suites. And that is important! But I believe it is also important for you to know how to secure your wireless network at home. I think you need to understand that you have choices when it comes to the applications you use. I believe you need to have at least a fundamental understanding of the grave security and privacy risks that RFID pose to you on a daily basis. My students find learning about the Deep Web and the Dark Net both interesting and a wee bit frightening, and I think you might too. I believe it is important that you preserve your privacy when you enter the Internet, and at the same time be able to recognize some of the formidable risks to your data and your identity that you are exposed to each time you fire up your browser. And finally, I have given you a 24-hour challenge. I have been giving my students this unique opportunity for several years now. I beg you to take that challenge, as every one of my students who mastered it found it both enlightening and enjoyable. Many have incorporated some version of it into their weekly or monthly schedule because they found that paying attention to people instead of devices is truly rewarding. Some even credit this challenge with strengthening their relationships with their spouse and family.

In a nutshell, I wrote this book because it contains things you really need to understand to live your digital life to its fullest, and at the same time, do so safely and privately.

One caution, however. Each of the topics I address in this book is rapidly changing. What you have here is a snapshot of these topics at the time I wrote this book. They provide you with a view of each concept, and enough background so you can pursue those that interest you further. Please stay current with these ideas as they affect your life in a plethora of ways. As these digital devices and ideas become more and more integrated into the fabric of our daily lives, we must always be conscious of both the benefits and the dangers they offer us. I hope you have as much fun learning about these amazing ideas as I have had studying and writing about them.

Stay safe, don't run with scissors, look both ways when you cross the street, and backup your data early and often!

Respectfully,
Telford

Securing Your Wireless Network

THE PROBLEM(S) WITH WIRELESS NETWORKS

Wireless networking technology gives us GREAT benefits. It makes it easy to move about the house while maintaining an Internet connection, and frees us from the constraints of cables and drilling holes in our walls, floors, and ceilings. It allows us to put devices where they make the most sense, not just where they have to be to be connected. And when you have set up a wireless network in your home, all your friends can log on and use your Internet connection easily. But, as with all other technology, if we don't do our due diligence when installing them, wireless networks also expose us to some unique and potentially very dangerous situations. Unfortunately, some ISPs (Internet Service Providers) assume that all their users know how, and are willing to, secure their networks from intrusion. For most of us, nothing could be further from the truth.

Let's look at how a wireless network looks:

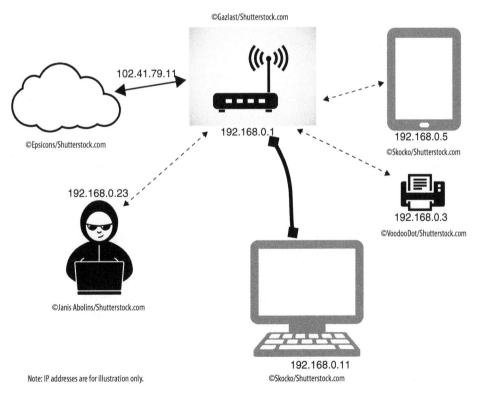

©Gazlast/Shutterstock.com

102.41.79.11

192.168.0.1

192.168.0.5

©Skocko/Shutterstock.com

©Epsicons/Shutterstock.com

192.168.0.23

192.168.0.3

©VoodooDot/Shutterstock.com

©Janis Abolins/Shutterstock.com

192.168.0.11

©Skocko/Shutterstock.com

Note: IP addresses are for illustration only.

Figure 1 A typical home wired/wireless network.

Let's take a close look at Figure 1. The figure contains a LOT of information, so let's take it one piece at a time.

Cloud: Starting at the top left, you see the cloud, and the arrow represents the connection between your router/modem and the Internet. Each node (end point of the network) on the Internet must have a unique IP (Internet Protocol) address. In this case, your ISP has assigned the IP address 102.41.79.11 to YOUR modem. Everything that goes to the Internet from your house or comes to your house from the Internet is associated with that, and only that, IP address.

Router: Your router/modem connects your home network to the cloud. That's what routers do. Interestingly, your router has a different address depending on which side of the router you look at it from. From the cloud, your router has the public address 102.41.79.11, like we saw in the preceding paragraph. BUT, from within your network, the router has the private address 192.168.0.1. (There are a few different private addresses your router can have from the inside, this one is the most common. 192.168.1.1 is another common address.) The documentation that comes with your router/modem will tell you what the internal or private IP address is. This is important, if you want to access your router from within your network, you have to use the private IP address.

Printer: Being terribly high-tech, you have a networked printer so you can print documents from any of your devices. This is especially handy when you are using your tablet or laptop. Each time you connect a device to your router, the router will assign that device a private IP address, but not necessarily the same private IP address the device had earlier. Using private IP addresses is one way the router can keep track of which device gets each piece of information coming in from the cloud. In the figure, your printer has the private IP address 192.168.0.5.

Desktop: Your desktop is hard-wired to your router. Since you are a serious game player, you want to be connected via ethernet, not wireless, because a hard-wired connection is MUCH faster! Even though you are hard-wired in, your router assigned you the private IP address 192.168.0.11. Each device connected to the router from inside your private network is given a 192.168.*.* address.

Bad Dude: Hmmmmm, looks like you have a BIG problem here. Somebody is accessing your network and you don't know it! You never gave him access, but there he is, using your network for who-knows-what! We will look at how to prevent this from happening in a few paragraphs. What is important now is that your router gave Bad Dude access and assigned him an internal IP address! What happens if that Bad Dude decides to do something illegal? What cloud (public) IP address would be associated with the bad stuff Bad Dude did? Yup, YOUR IP address (102.41.79.11) will show up as the offending address. What does that mean to you? Well, how will you prove that you didn't do the bad stuff? You can't! That's right, if Bad Dude did something illegal and left digital footprints, those footprints will lead right back to you! It will be difficult, if not impossible, for you to prove it wasn't you who committed the crime. It used to be a valid defense against prosecution if you explained that your router was not protected, and you didn't know who did what. Unfortunately, that is no longer a valid defense. The Internet community now holds you responsible for controlling access to your router. So, let's see what we can do to make your wireless network a wee bit more secure.

The first question is whether or not you currently need to enter a password to log into your network. If you don't, you are taking an extreme risk. If anyone can log in to your router without having to enter a password, then you can do very little to prevent them from logging in. So, let's do some things to make your wireless network more secure. Note: These techniques are divided into two sections; the first three are those you MUST do...today....right NOW. The suggestions after the first three will make your network more secure but will increase the hassle legitimate users encounter the first time they log into your network.

WHAT YOU MUST DO

1. Change the administrator password on your router. In most cases, the router manufacturer has set up both an administrator user ID and the password for that admin account. You can find the administrator username and password either in the documentation that came with your router, or on a sticker on the side or bottom of your router. Go find it right now. If you have lost the documentation for your router, you may be able to find the default admin user and password on a site like: **http://www.computerhome.com/ issues/ch001289.htm**
   That site lists many of the popular routers along with their default administrator username and password. Your humble author is concerned because so many of those passwords are "admin" or similar. Once you have your admin username and password, you can move on to finish this step.

   a. Log into your router, preferably from a hard-wired terminal as that is much more secure.

      1. You log into your router by typing the router's private address in the location bar of your router. For this section, I will be using the IP address 192.168.0.1, but your router may have a different private address. Check the documentation that came with your router. You should see a screen like that in Figure 2.

Figure 2   Login to Wireless Router.

b. Enter admin username and the default or factory password to sign into your router as the administrator. Now you can begin making changes.

c. Change the administrator password to a good, secure password. Something like V8k*9pR#&7 is a good choice. The password should have at least 8 characters, and should include both upper and lower case letters, numbers, and special characters. Don't make it easy to guess! If you don't do this first, and a black hat hacker breaks into your system, that hacker can do anything he wants, and undo everything you are about to do! Setting the admin password is the necessary first step. Because if you don't, it's easy for a BHH (Black Hat Hacker) to log into your system because there are websites that publish all the default administrator names and passwords. They do that, of course, to help you if you forget your default login information, you can find it and log into your router. A BHH would NEVER think of using those data to attack your router! (HA!, Right) Once the admin password is fixed, we are ready to move on to other changes. (Practical note: It's perfectly acceptable to put this hard-to-guess password on a post-it note and stick it to your modem/router. That's because if someone is able to physically access your router, they could reset it to the factory defaults by pushing the reset button. That would reset the password to the default password...and allow them access anyway.) Figure 3 shows you how it looks on my router.

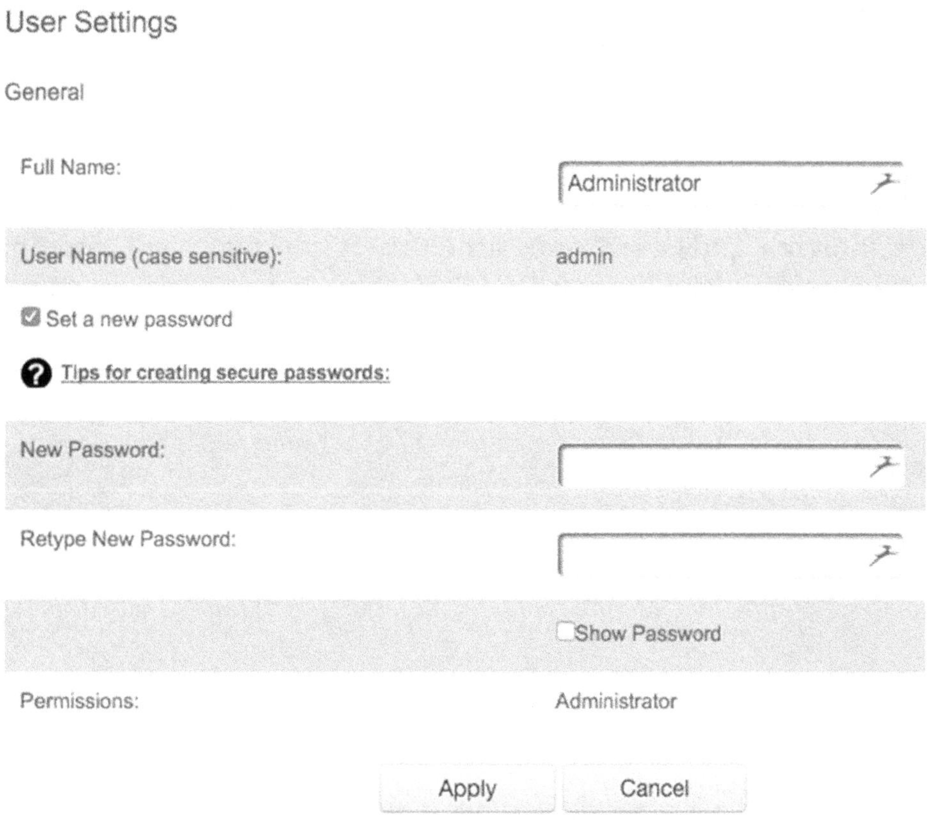

User Settings

General

Full Name: Administrator ✗

User Name (case sensitive):   admin

☑ Set a new password

❓ Tips for creating secure passwords:

New Password: ✗

Retype New Password: ✗

☐ Show Password

Permissions: Administrator

Apply   Cancel

Figure 3 Setting a new administrator password. Make it a good one!!.

2. Turn on encryption. Until you do this, all the data sent from your devices to the router/modem and back are sent "in the clear" or in what's called clear text. That means that anyone who can receive the radio signal from your router can do what is called packet sniffing to read the contents of all the data sent both ways. They can easily intercept all data sent across the network using any one of a number of freely available programs out there on the Net. There are three different encryption methods available that will make this much harder, if not impossible, for anyone to access:

a. WEP (Wireless Encryption Protocol). This is an older encryption methodology, and one that is somewhat more secure than clear text transmission, but not sufficient for our purposes. WEP is fairly weak encryption. A mildly serious black hat hacker should be able to break your WEP encryption in 60 seconds or less, using off-the-Net software. When I Googled "breaking WEP encryption" I got 102,000 results!

b. WPA (WiFi Protected Access) and WPA2. These encryption methodologies are much more secure and robust than WEP. Even with a good computer, it can take weeks, (or more!), to break a WPA password. Using this methodology, each user must provide a password that signifies their authorization to use the network. That password is then turned into a key unique to their device. The key is used to encrypt the clear text, creating ciphertext. Then the ciphertext is broadcast to and from the device. If a black hat hacker packet sniffs these packets all they can see are the encrypted data. This password, or pass phrase, needs to be long, and UGLY! Remember, anyone using your network will only have to enter this ugly, horrible password once since their computer will remember it. Do make it really ugly! I mean REALLY ugly! Figure 4 shows how my router

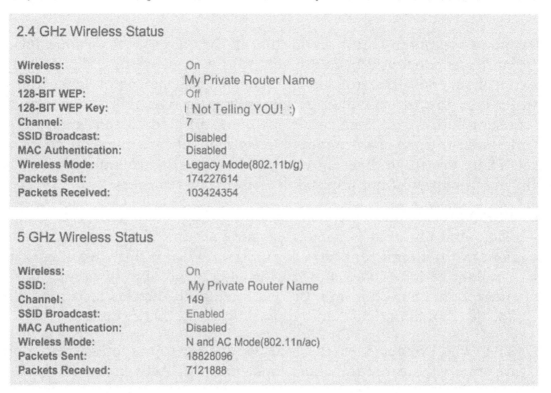

Password Tips:
Use a mix of letters and numbers. Don't use personal information that could be guessed or easily discovered (for example, names of family members, birthdates, phone numbers)

2.4 GHz Wireless

Select a WEP Key: 128/104 bit

ASCII

Key Code: ! Not Telling YOU! :)
0 Digits Left

6. Write down wireless settings.
In order for every computer to connect to this Router wirelessly, you need to make sure that the wireless setup for each computer uses the SAME settings listed below. Please make sure that you write down all of the values set on this screen.

2.4 GHz Wireless Status

Wireless:	On
SSID:	My Private Router Name
128-BIT WEP:	Off
128-BIT WEP Key:	! Not Telling YOU! :)
Channel:	7
SSID Broadcast:	Disabled
MAC Authentication:	Disabled
Wireless Mode:	Legacy Mode(802.11b/g)
Packets Sent:	174227614
Packets Received:	103424354

5 GHz Wireless Status

Wireless:	On
SSID:	My Private Router Name
Channel:	149
SSID Broadcast:	Enabled
MAC Authentication:	Disabled
Wireless Mode:	N and AC Mode(802.11n/ac)
Packets Sent:	18828096
Packets Received:	7121888

Figure 4   This shows where I can set my "Key Code" or encryption key. Note: It says "WEP" on the screen, but actually, this is a WPA2 key.

setup for a WPA password works. Notice that under that section, you can see some of the data about how my router is configured. I have masked the SSID and the WPA key. Big surprise, huh? LOL (Note, there is an error in the administrator screens here, it says "WEP Key" but I have turned off WEP. This is really my WPA2 key. They need to update their software!)

3. Change the name of your router/network. Your router was given a name by the manufacturer. That name is often the identifier for all routers of that particular type. Another term for the name of your network is SSID (Service Set IDentifier). For example, if your router/network is called "LinkSys-A23" then anyone who can see your router knows exactly what kind of router it is! You can go online, for example to the site referenced in point one of this section, and see what the default administrator ID and password are. Knowing that, a black hat hacker can attempt to log into, and control, your entire network! That's why your first step was to change the administrator password. If you change the name of your router to something like "phred," or "Phil's Huge Network," anyone who can see your network has no idea what hardware you are using. That makes it nearly impossible to find out what the default access is since there is no way of knowing who built the router!

   This router broadcasts on two different frequencies to reduce the number of users on any one frequency. I could have given the two frequencies different names if I wanted to keep one all to myself!

Note: Some of the manufacturers of high power, specialty routers have begun to address these problems. Your humble author's new router had a unique name, and the default password was a long, ugly string of characters that is supposed to be unique to this particular, individual, router. Of course he trusts the manufacturer and hasn't "fixed" the name and key! Oh SURE he does! :)

Basic Security Settings

Instructions for setting up a wireless network using basic WEP wireless security are set out below. However, we recommend that you establish stronger security using the Advanced Security Settings. To establish stronger security, select "OFF" in Step 4, click on APPLY and then go to Advanced Security Settings to setup security.

1. Turn Wireless On

2.4 GHz Wireless:	● On	○ Off	5 GHz Wireless:	● On	○ Off

2. Change the SSID setting to any name or code you want
(SSID is the same thing as the name of your Wireless Network.)

2.4 GHz SSID:	I won't tell you!	5 GHz SSID:	I still won't tell you LOL

Figure 5   Setting a new SSID.

You MUST do the three (3) things above this line!!!! NOW!!!!!!

You may choose to do some or all of the following steps to increase the security of your network. Be SURE to do the first 3 steps as soon as possible!

The following steps will each make your home network more and more secure. In addition, they will make your home network more difficult to access for legitimate first time users. If you are living in a very population-dense environment, however, you may well wish to implement the next couple of steps.

4. Turn off Guest Access. Most routers have a default "guest" username that anyone is allowed to use. This might be handy if you are running an ice cream store and want to give your customers access to your wireless network, but it presents a danger to your home network. A black hat hacker could use guest access to attack your network from inside. Obviously, if your router doesn't have guest access, you won't have to worry about it at all. Just be sure your router doesn't allow guest access. Note: All the routers I have worked with turn off guest access by default. If you have inherited your router from someone else, or if you suspect that someone has been playing

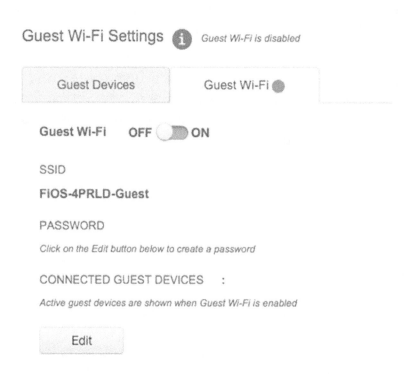

Figure 6   Disabling Guest access.

with your router, you should be sure to check this and turn off guest access if it happens to be turned on.

5. Turn off SSID broadcast. The SSID is just another way to refer to the name of your network. Remember, back in step three, you changed the name of your network from the one the Figure 6 Showing that Guest access is disabled. Had it been on, I would turn it off here.

   If you turn off SSID broadcast, then only people who know the name of your network will be able to access it. It will NOT show up in the "pick a network to connect to" list when someone tries to find a wireless network to connect to. The down side of this is that when people come to your house for the first time, you will have to tell them the network name, and they will have to select the correct option on their WiFi connection screen. On that screen they will have to type in the name of your network. Again, this should only happen the very first time they connect to your network as their computer should remember that network name from then on.

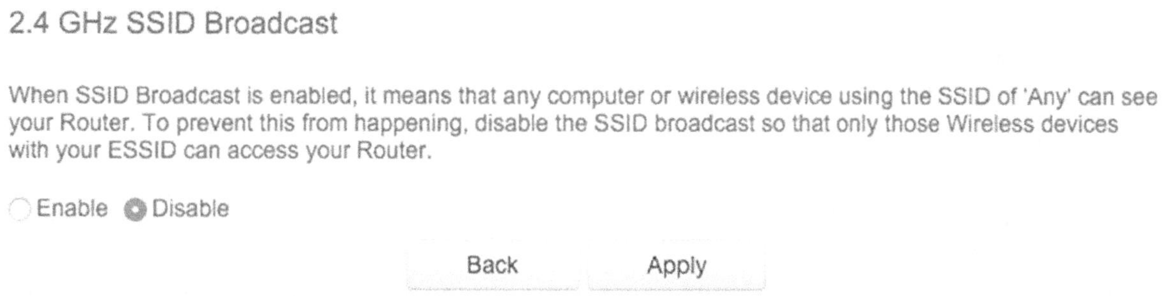

2.4 GHz SSID Broadcast

When SSID Broadcast is enabled, it means that any computer or wireless device using the SSID of 'Any' can see your Router. To prevent this from happening, disable the SSID broadcast so that only those Wireless devices with your ESSID can access your Router.

○ Enable ● Disable

Back   Apply

Figure 7   Showing that SSID broadcast is turned off. Had it been on, I would disable it here.

6. Reduce the broadcast strength. Some routers allow you to set the strength of the signal they broadcast. If you live in a reasonably small apartment, or if you live in a house with small lots, you probably don't need to provide WiFi access to your neighbors. The signal from your router needs to be strong enough to give you good signal strength anywhere you want to use your computer. But, do you really need to access your network from the other side of the road from your house? Or do you need to access your network three floors above your apartment? WiFi piggybacking is, unfortunately all too common, and anything anyone does on your network is your responsibility! My router doesn't have this feature, probably because

I bought this particular router because it had a larger range...i.e. stronger broadcast strength!

7. Turn on MAC address filtering. This is the most extreme step you can take to protect your network from assault. It is also the step that will cause you the most hassle the first time a new, legitimage user tries to access your network. If you have performed the first 5 steps in this section, you should be relatively well-protected. If you want to absolutely make sure that no one except the chosen few have access to your network, you can perform this last step. The MAC or Media Access Control address is a 12-digit hexadecimal number that is physically stored in each NIC (Network Interface Card) when it is manufactured. The first set of six hexadecimal digits identify the manufacturer of the device, the next set of six hexadecimal digits are a unique serial number. The combination of the two ensure that each and every NIC has a unique MAC address. Your router knows the MAC address of each device connected to it, and uses those addresses to route data to a specific device. You can specify that only known MAC addresses may connect to the router or ban specific MAC address from connecting, regardless of any of the previous steps. (Note: a determined black hat hacker could possibly engage in "MAC address spoofing," so this step, by itself, is not sufficient to protect your network.) This step makes allowing someone new access to your network a much bigger hassle. You will have to log into your router as the administrator, and then manually enter the new device's MAC address into the table of allowed addresses. To do that you must, of course, know the MAC address of the new hardware. As with the other steps in this process, you only have to enter the MAC address once. From then on the router will remember the address and allow or prevent connection by that device. (Note: Usually the only time you would block specific MAC addresses would be if one of your network users needed to be prevented from using the Net. For example, my son doesn't want his four-year old son to have free access to the Net. Therefore, he blocks the iPad my grandson uses.)

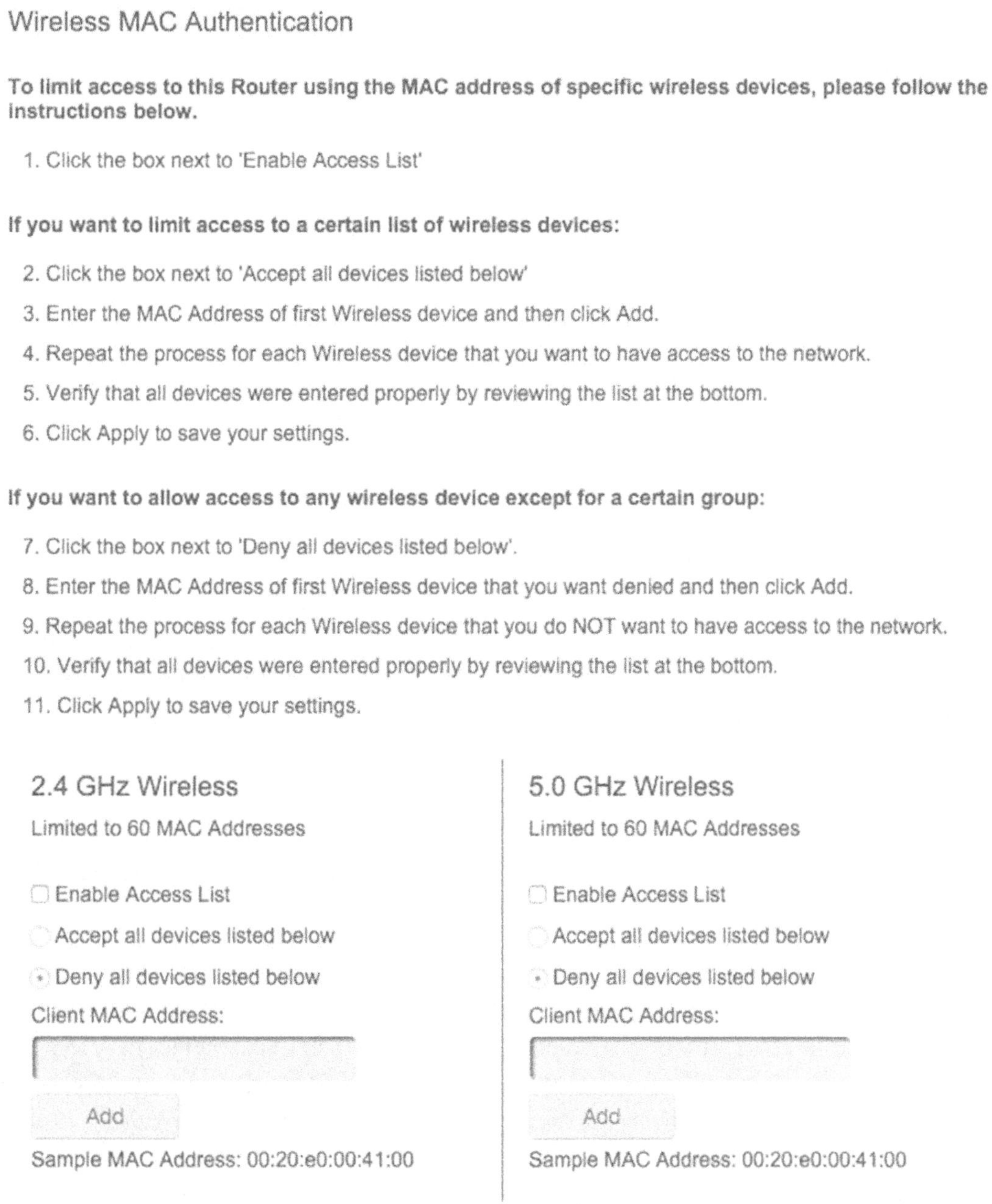

Wireless MAC Authentication

To limit access to this Router using the MAC address of specific wireless devices, please follow the instructions below.

1. Click the box next to 'Enable Access List'

If you want to limit access to a certain list of wireless devices:

2. Click the box next to 'Accept all devices listed below'

3. Enter the MAC Address of first Wireless device and then click Add.

4. Repeat the process for each Wireless device that you want to have access to the network.

5. Verify that all devices were entered properly by reviewing the list at the bottom.

6. Click Apply to save your settings.

If you want to allow access to any wireless device except for a certain group:

7. Click the box next to 'Deny all devices listed below'.

8. Enter the MAC Address of first Wireless device that you want denied and then click Add.

9. Repeat the process for each Wireless device that you do NOT want to have access to the network.

10. Verify that all devices were entered properly by reviewing the list at the bottom.

11. Click Apply to save your settings.

2.4 GHz Wireless	5.0 GHz Wireless
Limited to 60 MAC Addresses	Limited to 60 MAC Addresses
☐ Enable Access List	☐ Enable Access List
○ Accept all devices listed below	○ Accept all devices listed below
◉ Deny all devices listed below	◉ Deny all devices listed below
Client MAC Address:	Client MAC Address:
[ ]	[ ]
Add	Add
Sample MAC Address: 00:20:e0:00:41:00	Sample MAC Address: 00:20:e0:00:41:00

Figure 8 This is the screen I would use to enter the MAC address of each device I wanted to allow (or block) and I am limited to 60 addresses.

Now, a quick recap of the three things you have to do this very day!

I. Change the administrator password. Make it UGLY! You can put it on a Post-It note on the side of your router.

II. Turn on WPA or WPA2 encryption and set a really ugly, long key. It will only need to be input once per user, so even a REALLY long key will be good. Mine is a randomly generated string of 13 letters and numbers.

III. Change the SSID of your router.

Those three things need to be done as soon as you are able to. In the next 10 minutes wouldn't be too soon!

What about out in public?????

OK, so now your personal WiFi network is secure...good for you! But what about those times when you have to use somebody else's WiFi network? Like when you go to a restaurant or coffee shop and they have "free WiFi" for their customers? Can you expect them to have secured their network like you have secured yours? Nope! They are in the business of selling a product, be it coffee or a meal, so they want you to be able to access their network easily and efficiently. It's up to you to be smart, and safe, using their network. There are five steps you should implement to be secure while using a public WiFi network. The first of these is the most complex, and you will need to do a little research on it. I have provided some links to help you pick the best service for your particular needs (see the glossary). So what do you need to do to be safe on a public network?

1. Implement a Virtual Private Network (VPN). Yes, this will require you do to a little bit of research, and to understand a bit about the various VPN services. Don't just automatically pick the cheapest one. You do get what you pay for. A VPN is like creating a little personal, encrypted, private network connection between you and the rest of the world. It will prevent anyone from being able to decipher what you are using your computer for, and will also enable you to securely conduct your business in a public place. If you don't choose to do this, please don't do anything personal like look at your Facebook page, do any banking, do any purchasing, etc. on that public network. In other words, if you don't implement a VPN, restrict your public usage to sites where you don't need to log in.

2. Use two-factor authentication. This is also very important. Two factor authentication means that there are two different steps you must complete before you can log into a website. To give you an example, when I try to log into my Gmail account I must provide my username and password (one factor), then the Gmail server sends a text message with a code to my phone. I must next enter that code (the second factor), before I can log into my Gmail account. That means that even if a hacker steals my Gmail password, he/she can't log into my account unless they steal my phone as well. Another example is my PayPal account. There I also need to log in using my username and password, the first factor. But then, I have to enter a special number that is available on my PayPal security key. This security key is a credit-card-sized device that contains a little computer that generates a pseudo-random string of numbers. Each time I use the security key, it generates a new number. The PayPal site uses the same pseudo-random number generator to generate a, hopefully, matching number. Since both devices have the same algorithm, and start with the same number, the PayPal site can verify that the number I enter is one that has not been used before, and is one from the list of possible numbers my security key can generate. If the number generated by the processor in my security key matches one of the unused numbers generated by the PayPal site, I am allowed to log in. Once a number is used it cannot be reused so even if a hacker sees my username, password, and the verification number, they can't reuse that number. That means that, should a hacker steal my PayPal password and user ID, they are prevented from accessing my account unless they also steal my security key.

3. Be careful about allowing your device to automatically reconnect to a server. While it is handy for your device to automatically remember and reconnect to a previously known hot spot, that practice is dangerous. If a hacker creates a spoof hot spot using the same SSID as, say, your local coffee shop, your device may connect to that hot spot instead of the correct server. Then the hacker could monitor all your communications, capture everything you do, and in some cases even log into your computer and steal data. By the same token, you should prevent all of your devices that work as a hot spot, like your mobile phone, from displaying their SSID. Not broadcasting your SSID is much more important when you are outside your home. We discussed this in point four above when we were looking at securing your home network.

4. Verify the network. You need to be sure that the network you are connecting to IS the network you think it is. It is easy for a hacker to set up a computer to pretend to be the target router, capture and analyze your connection data (names and passwords), and then pass you on to the actual site, often supplying your login information. From that point on everything you enter, and everything you see, will pass through the hacker's hot spot. He/she can then record everything you do and see. This type of hack is called a "man-in-the-middle" attack. One

way to verify that the site you are connecting to displays the special lock icon in the location bar. It is difficult for a hacker to spoof that icon.

5. Don't log in! If possible, when you are in public, avoid using sites that require you to log in. Use only open websites like Google that allow access without a login. Don't go to your Gmail account, don't buy things, don't go to your bank, just don't use any site that requires your login. If you really must log in, please restrict your access to sites that support HTTPS protocol. That way all the information you send is encrypted at your browser so communications between your browser and the website are encrypted before a hacker can even see it. While this is good....not loggin' in at all is MUCH better! Really, you can wait until you are in a safe place, now can't you?

GLOSSARY

Term	Definition
Clear Text	The term used by the encryption community to describe data that have not been encrypted. Clear text can be easily read by anyone who can see the data stream from and/or to the router. That means that if you log into your bank using an unencrypted network, anyone can easily see and steal your private information. Transmitting personal or financial data in clear text is very dangerous.
Ciphertext	Ciphertext is data that have been encrypted. Trying to read ciphertext without the key to the encryption is very difficult, and usually impossible for most hackers.
MAC Address	The MAC (Media Access Control) address is a physical address for a NIC, (Network Interface Card). Every NIC must have a unique MAC address. This address is built into the device during the manufacturing process and is not designed to be changed. The format of the MAC address is usually shown as: MM:MM:MM:SS:SS:SS where the Ms are six hexadecimal digits (24 bits) that identify the manufacturer and the specific type of NIC. The Ss in the MAC address are a unique, six-digit serial number for that specific device. This combination of the 12 hexadecimal digits (creates a unique, 48-bit address for each NIC. As an example, the MAC address of the wireless NIC on my iMac is 7C:6D:62:73:82:69. By the way, the term MAC had nothing to do with Apple! :)

Term	Definition
Packet Sniffing	Describes the technique of capturing data moving across a network. Packet sniffing is a very simple process and there are many open source programs available that enable packet sniffing. From a network administrator's point of view, packet sniffing is a very valuable diagnostic tool. From your point of view, it is a serious liability.
Private IP address	Private IP addressing was developed to help handle the huge number of devices that want to be connected to the Internet. This system sets aside a range of IP addresses that can only be accessed from inside a network. The range of private IP addresses is 192.168.0.0 – 192.168.255.255, which gives 65,536 possible private addresses. When a device on a private network wants to communicate with another device on that same network, the two devices can use the private IP address. However, when any of those devices wants to communicate with the Net, or any device outside the private network, that device must use the public IP address of the router/modem.
Public IP address	A public IP address is one of the block of the addresses assigned by either ICANN, or more recently IANA (Internet Assigned Numbers Authority) to your ISP. Your ISP then assigns one address from that block of numbers to your router/modem. Any traffic across the Net from your private network will show up as coming from that one public IP address. It works like your postal address the mail comes to, and goes out from, your mailbox. Once the mail is delivered, someone can distribute the individual letters to the people they are addressed to. Your router/modem sends and receives information from the Net via the public IP address. Then it will deliver the content sent to any specific device within your private network directly to that device.
SSID	Service Set IDentifier. This is just the publicly-visible name for your router, or the network you are attaching to. Router manufacturers generally provide a default SSID that identifies the manufacturer and possibly the model of router. If you do not change that identifier, it will be much easier for a nefarious outsider to guess the default administrator ID and password. Of course you have, or will shortly, change the administrator ID and password, but changing the SSID adds another level of hardening to your network.

Term	Definition
VPN	Virtual Private Network. To put it simply, you are creating a secure, encrypted connection between your device (cell phone or computer), and another network. Because the connection is encrypted, it's like you are sitting at the target network's home base. Using a VPN ensures that your communications in a wireless environment are relatively secure. Some texts reference a VPN "tunnel," (the term for the encrypted connection you make, it's sorta like a tunnel for your data because it prevents anyone from spying on you and seeing just what characters you send). Most of the time users purchase a VPN service which handles the communications for you. It is really a good investment if you frequently use public WiFi networks...and most of us do! :) Here is a review of the more widely used VPN packages as done by PC Magazine: http://www.pcmag.com/article2/0,2817,2403388,00.asp And if you have a Mac: https://www.bestvpn.com/blog/31943/5-best-vpns-mac-november-2015-update/ As I have been writing this book, I have researched many VPN tools. I have found the one that I think is the best, especially for the price. This is the VPN I am now using! www.saferweb.com You might want to check it out!

Autonomous Vehicles

What is an autonomous vehicle? Well, other names for them are: self-driving vehicle, driver-less vehicle, robot vehicle, and un-crewed vehicle. These are vehicles that are capable of sensing and reacting to changes in their environment. Autonomous cars and trucks will use existing roads to transport their load from point A to point B. Truly autonomous military drones might be able not only to seek out a target to surveil, but in the worst case also decide, with no human guidance, which targets to eliminate! The critical thing is that autonomous devices perform their functions with little or no human intervention! The machine, JUST the machine, is making the decisions. (Well, to be technical about it, the algorithms (programs) controlling the machines are really making the decision. The important thing is that at the time of the decision there is no human to approve or override it.)

The path to a truly self-driving or smart car has been and probably will continue to be, a fairly long one. Automobiles have gradually become more and more "intelligent." What does "smarter" mean right now, it means becoming better able to assist the driver in performing the many tasks involved in driving. However, it is a major leap to go from a car that assists the driver to one that is completely independent of human guidance. The biggest challenge isn't the technology, we are making great strides on that front. The real problem comes from

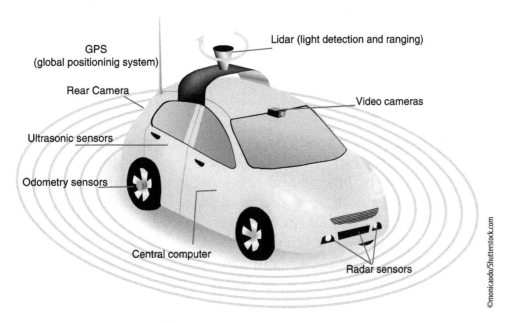

Figure 1 An autonomous car....sort of.

the algorithms the vehicle will use to decide which of several possible actions it should take. We will look at a couple of those ethical questions a bit later in this section.

The first thing we need to consider is the reason(s) driving (pun intended) the development of an autonomous vehicle. For this discussion we will only consider automobiles, since those are the vehicle most of us will most often interact with. Why build cars that help, or replace the driver? The tantamount reason is safety. An estimated 1.3 MILLION people a year die in traffic accidents. Many of these accidents are caused by human error or stupidity. Stupidity in that to choose to drive drunk, exhausted, over medicated, etc. is a stupid decision and yet lots of people make those decisions. Since robots can't get drunk, tired, over medicated, or stupid....(well, that last one is up for grabs)...having them in control of the car should make it safer. A robotic car will react to changes in the driving environment much more quickly than a human. The "reaction time" of a computer is much faster than that of a person. The average human reaction time in the U.S. is 2.3 seconds. That means it will take 2.3 seconds from the time the driver recognizes a problem that requires her to brake, until the time when she begins to depresses the brake pedal. If she is traveling at 60 miles per hour, that means her car will cover just over 200 feet before she starts pressing the brake pedal! (60 miles / hour is 1 mile per minute. A mile is 5280 feet. 5280 divided by 60 seconds is equal to 88 feet. 88 ft / second times 2.3 seconds is equal to 202.4 feet.) So, in a situation where, say, the car in front of her slams on the brakes, an augmented car, "smart" car, could theoretically stop more quickly. If another car begins to move into your lane, a "smart" car should be able to sense that and warn you, or avoid the encroaching car. The list goes on and on. Let's look at some the ways cars are beginning to become "smarter."

SEMI-SMART CARS

The fact is, you most likely already have a semi-smart car. Nearly all the cars on the road today have "anti-lock" brakes. You see, you can stop the car in a shorter distance if you "pump" the brakes and prevent the tires from skidding. If the tires keep rolling, instead of skidding, you can still steer the car. Being able to steer is often critical if you want to avoid an accident. If you have the unfortunate necessity to slam on your brakes, you will notice that the brake peddle begins vibrating, (and it makes an awful noise!). That vibration is your anti-lock brakes preventing the tires from stopping rotation and skidding. What exactly is happening? When you apply the brakes, the computer in your car begins to monitor the rotation of your wheels. If one, or more, of the wheels begins to lose traction and start skidding, the computer opens a valve in the hydraulic line reducing the strength of the braking force on that wheel. That way your wheels keep rolling, and you maintain your ability to steer the car. If, on the other hand, your brakes "lock up" your tires will skid, and regardless of how you turn the wheel, physics will see to it that your car continues in a nice, straight line....Probably NOT what you want to happen. Ouch!

A more recent addition to braking technology is called Adaptive Braking. It adds features to the anti-lock brakes by also trying to anticipate when braking will be necessary. Using both front and rear RADAR the adaptive braking system adds pressure to the brake system when it detects your car coming closer to an object, usually a car, in front of you. That way, when you decide to brake, the system is much more responsive. Some versions of adaptive braking will even apply the brakes if the system thinks a collision is imminent and you haven't begun to brake. Having "smart" brakes also makes it easier to start from a stop on a hill without rolling backward. Some systems will automatically apply the brakes to hold the car stationary until you press the accelerator enough to get the car moving forward.

Another fairly early "smart" thing cars already do is to change the volume of the stereo based upon the vehicle's speed. As you drive faster, the car generates more noise. Wind noise, engine noise, transmission noise, tires on the road noise, and occasionally the noise of blaring horns when you cut someone off. :) This feature gradually raises or lowers the volume of the stereo/radio to maintain good sound quality regardless of the speed of the vehicle.

A relatively old "smart" technology is cruise control. By accelerating to the desired speed, and turning on the cruise control the car will try to maintain that speed from then on. That is a really handy option on a long trip over a lightly traveled road. You can, figuratively, sit back and just steer the car, trusting that the computer will keep it moving at a constant speed. That's all well and good until the car in front of you slows down. Your cruise control will keep your car going at the set speed until it crashes into the car in front, or until you disable cruise control, usually by touching the brake or clutch pedal. Robots (dare I say autobots?) to the rescue! Newer versions of cruise control, called adaptive cruise control, active cruise control, autonomous cruise control, intelligent cruise control, or RADAR cruise control take things a step further. Using the same RADAR system that adaptive braking uses, autonomous cruise control lets you set the desired top speed, but adjusts your actual speed to that of the car(s) in front of you. If they slow down, your car automatically slows to keep a safe distance between you and the car you are following. If the car in front of you speeds up, your car will accelerate as well, while still keeping a safe distance from the car in front. As the traffic moves faster, your car will continue to accelerate up to your specified maximum speed. The same thing will happen if you move out from behind the slow car into an empty lane. Sensing no car in the near distance, usually about 500 feet maximum, adaptive cruise control will accelerate your car back up to your chosen speed. At the time of this writing, there are already over 25 vehicles that come equipped with adaptive cruise control. Among them are the 2016 Lexus ES 350, the 2015 Volvo S60, the 2016 Hyundai Genesis, the 2016 Audi A6 and the 2015 Toyota Highlander Hybrid.

Starting in 2010, most automobiles have been equipped with a kind of "black box" called a telemetric device. It's similar to the black box or flight data recorder in airplanes that records all sorts of in-flight information like the altitude, navigational heading, speed, etc. Airplane black boxes (which are actually painted bright orange) are valuable in the event of an aircraft crash because they give the investigators data about exactly what happened to the plane just before the crash. Automotive black boxes initially did pretty much the same thing. They recorded about five seconds of data and measured the speed, rate of deceleration, whether there was an impact, how many impacts there were, and whether or not the airbag deployed. Those data were sometimes useful in crash investigations. Since the data were constantly re-written they were of value only in an accident situation. However, things have changed in the last year or so!

The change was instituted by insurance companies. You see, there is great competition among different car insurance companies, just note the number of insurance ads on television. And the business of insurance companies is to make money. They make money when they receive more in premiums than they have to pay out in claims. So how do they reduce the number of claims? Enter the new telemetric devices. Insurance companies currently offer the carrot of reduced premiums if you place one of their black boxes on your vehicle. What THIS black box monitors is: acceleration, deceleration, average speed, top speed, and cornering. Some also have a GPS that keeps track of where you drive. The idea being that if you know that your car is monitoring you, and reporting back to the insurance company if you drive more...ahem...assertively, you will start driving like a little old lady. Some of these new back seat drivers even beep to tell you when you are doing something wrong! For now, the insurance companies claim that these data will not be used to raise the premiums of drivers who actually like to drive their cars, and will only be used to lower the premiums of what they consider "good" drivers. Sure, you bet. In addition to reporting to the insurance companies, these data can also be shared with the driver, or...the drivers parents! Now I am sure these Little Brothers, (see 1984 by George Orwell) are great for some people. However, as I learned to drive race cars in my mis-spent youth, and still have a tendency to drive a wee bit, um, shall we say assertively, I think that having my car telling me how to drive is perverse. Another frightening question is whether these Orwellian spies will be required to even get car insurance in the future! These vulgar devices make your car smart enough to snoop on your driving habits and then tattle tale to your insurance company and possibly you parents. Yuck! And remember, some of them have GPS receivers installed, so they can also report exactly where the car was driven! Drivers beware, your beloved car could be turned into an evil spy instead of a source of genuine pleasure.

In concert with adaptive cruise control, there are two more "smart" features available on some cars. The first is lane departure warning. This technology uses a pair of cameras to watch your car's position in a lane, and warn you if the car begins drifting to the right or left. An addition to this technology is called lane keep assist which gently guides your car back into its lane if the system detects that you are about to cross a lane marker and you don't correct your path. This works provided, of course, that you haven't put on your turn signal indicating a lane change. If nothing else, these systems will force "blinker challenged" drivers to start using their turn signals before they move from lane to lane across traffic.

Another recent and valuable addition to your car's intelligence is called blind spot detection. This is another pair of cameras, one on each side of your car, that watch for vehicles coming up behind you on either rear quadrant. When a vehicle enters your "blind spot", the system warns you either with a sound, a visual display, or both.

In Figure 2, the grey areas are places where you can't see using your mirrors, so they are referred to as blind spots, since in those spots you are blind, duh! The solid

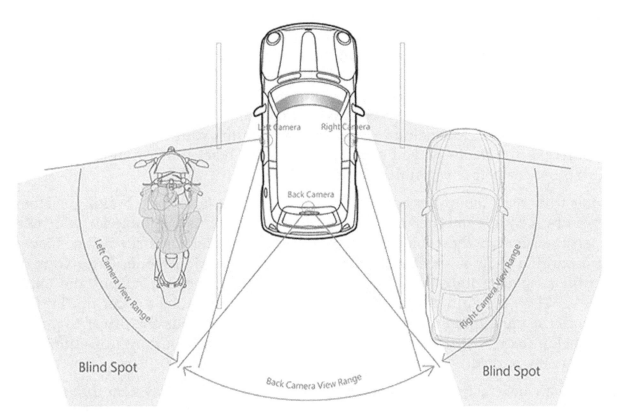

Figure 2 Blind spots in most automobiles (Source yankodesign.com).

lines in the image indicate the area that is "watched" by the blind spot detection system. Another type of blind spot detection uses RADAR to alert the driver if they are going to back into or over an object or person immediately behind the vehicle.

So how does a car "see?" Intelligent cars will use three complimentary systems to sense the world around them. First they use front and rear long range RADAR. That is what allows things like adaptive cruise control and adaptive braking. Next they have cameras. They need a rear camera, also called a backup camera to help you see behind the vehicle. They also need blind-spot cameras to keep you from changing lanes into a vehicle you can't see. Lane control uses small cameras that can detect the traffic lane lines painted on the road. They use short range RADAR to detect objects close to the car, for example a small child standing behind your vehicle as you begin to back up. That short range RADAR, often referred to as ultrasonic RADAR also comes into play if you have automatic parking. One of the newer sensors is Light Detection and Ranging (LiDAR.) LiDAR systems have a wide range of applications from weather detection to forest surveys. There is an article referenced at the end of this section that details 50 different ways LiDAR can be used. A LiDAR sensor sends out approximately 2.8 million laser pulses per second and calculates the time it takes for that light to return to the sensors on the unit. Since a LiDAR system employs light beyond the visible spectrum, your "smart" car can see in the dark. This is important because many traffic accidents occur after the sun goes down. According to the American Automobile Association fatal automobile accidents are four times more likely to happen at night. According to the National Highway Traffic Safety Administration most accidents occur between six and nine PM. LiDAR equipped vehicles can see further down the road than humans can, so they detect and react to objects in the roadway much more quickly than a human driver. One serious cause of night time accidents is over-driving the headlights. That means going so fast that by the time your headlights let you see an object in the roadway, you are so close to the object that you don't have time to stop the car before you hit the object.

Along with ACC (adaptive cruise control), and ABS (anti-lock braking system), there are a couple of other interesting "smart" additions available for your car's repertoire. One of the coolest, which has been around for a few years now, is auto-parking. This is most often used in parallel parking mode. Once your car identifies an acceptable parking space, it signals the driver to put the car in reverse. Then the auto-parking feature takes over and backs the car until it is as close to the car behind as reasonable. Then the system tells the driver to put the car back into drive and the system makes the next pass. This continues until your car is safely parked.

A relatively new technology is called "drive by wire." This is a system that replaces the old mechanical linkage between your steering wheel and your front wheels. Instead of a solid, mechanical connection that directly links the movement of your wheels to the movement of your steering wheel, this system uses sensors that pick up the movements of your steering wheel. The sensors send the steering wheel movement data to a steering force actuator. The actuator then sends commands to the electronic control unit (ECU.) The steering ECU sends signals to the steering angle actuator which actually turns the wheels. Although steer by wire is new for cars, it has been the norm in airplanes for many years. According to the research, in most cases drive by wire allows the car to be more responsive, and will eliminate the vibrations of the tires on the road that are transmitted by the current mechanical system. You won't have to "feel the road" anymore. Note: For some of us, feeling the road is an important part of driving, but these cars aren't designed for people who love to drive. We will see more about the implications of this and other "smart" technology shortly.

Many of the cars on the road already have "accelerate by wire" so drive by wire is a logical extension. In the good old days, when you mashed the accelerator to the floor, a mechanical linkage physically opened up the carburetor, increased the fuel flow, and away you went! Zoom. Speed control like this is almost completely reliable, giving the driver direct and absolute control of acceleration. With accelerate by wire, when you stomp on the gas pedal, a signal is sent to the Electronic Control Unit which evaluates the accelerator pedal position and sends data to a little motor that opens up the throttle body making your car go faster. All of this is, of course, is under the control of your ECU, which can, and usually does, limit just how fast you accelerate. For example, a Volkswagen I test drove, used a system to prevent spinning the tires when accelerating from a stop. When I tried to zip out into traffic, the system decided that I was accelerating too quickly. So it didn't give me the acceleration I asked for. Instead it rather smoothly, and SLOWLY, moved the car forward. Since I had expected much faster acceleration, I was nearly hit by oncoming traffic. Sometimes smart cars can be really dumb! Needless to say I didn't buy that particular VW.

There is even an application that is sometimes called the "Beep of Impending Doom." That is a system that will signal the driver when it detects an unavoidable collision is about to happen. Besides warning the driver, most systems will also tension the seat belts, begin to apply the brakes, or in some cases apply the brakes, and even reposition the seats for maximum airbag deployment. All of these steps are designed to help the driver survive the imminent and unavoidable accident.

The question becomes, "Why would anyone want an autonomous car?" Well, there are a lot of reasons. Some of the reasons are listed above, I mean, who wouldn't want a car that parks itself? Who wouldn't want a car with anti-lock brakes? (Actually, you would be hard pressed to find a car without that particular feature). But, those aren't really autonomous cars. Those are little features to make your driving experience safer and more convenient. It is a huge step from a car that can help you park to one that completely takes over the driving experience. The following are reasons why there is such a large effort underway to develop a truly autonomous car.

1. **Safety:** Yup, that is the number one reason why there is such a push to get cars that can monitor the driving environment and intervene quickly to handle potential problems. On average, 1.3 MILLION people die in road accidents each year. One million three hundred thousand people! Holy Cow! If self-driving cars could cut that by even 10%, that would save thousands of lives. (To be exact, 130,000 lives.) Remember, that figure doesn't take into account the 20-50 million people that are disabled or injured in vehicle accidents annually. That is a powerful reason to get autonomous vehicles out on the roads as soon as possible, isn't it?

2. **Traffic Congestion:** When true self-driving cars are developed, they will also communicate with the vehicles around them, almost completely eliminating "rush hour" gridlock since all the cars will maintain proper spacing, and none will over brake. Research by mathematicians at the University of Exeter have shown that if just one driver over brakes in response to a situation, say a car pulling into traffic from the shoulder of the road, that event can propagate backward through the traffic in what's called a "backward traveling wave." That wave can flow many miles back through traffic. As the wave moves backward, drivers are forced to brake more quickly and harder in response to the car in front of them braking. This often results in traffic coming to a complete stop miles back from the original incident. When those drivers finally move forward, they find they are in a traffic jam that has no visible cause. As the researchers reported, "overreaction of a single driver can have enormous impact on the rest of traffic, leading to massive delays."[i] Self-driving cars would most likely eliminate overreaction, and so would allow traffic to move more smoothly, and more importantly, much more quickly. Would it bother you to be in heavy traffic if it were moving at reasonable speed and didn't delay you? I think not. Note: If you are really into the actual physics/psychology of this kind of traffic jam, check out the article by Riener and Ferscha entitled, "Effect of Proactive Braking on Traffic Flow and Road Throughput." The reference to this study is in the "For Further Research" at the end of this section. To further help with traffic flow, some researchers are working on communications systems that allow vehicles to communicate with one another up and down the traffic stream. That kind of communications network will provide real-time traffic data. That way all the cars in a given traffic pattern can adjust their speed and spacing anticipating events on the road ahead.

3. **Economy:** Since self-driving cars wouldn't have as many hard braking/fast accelerating incidents, they would be much more fuel efficient (as well as

more boring.) And it's well known that your car is more fuel efficient if you drive at a consistent speed. There is even thought of developing a fleet of autonomous taxi like cars that a user could just call up to take them from point A to point B. Many people who live in dense metropolitan areas don't own cars, and have never even learned to drive. These folks rely on mass transit and taxis to move about rather than owning and driving their own cars. Car sharing companies like Uber, Lyft, Sidecar, and Flywheel allow users to "order up" rides. Uber is already testing autonomous cars which they hope will someday replace human driven cars. How does this work? To use Uber you to use an app on your smart phone to request a pickup up place and time and pay for a ride. Then the Uber system dispatches the nearest available car to pick you up and take you where you are going. The Uber model employs a number of volunteer, independent contractors, driving their own vehicles. The driver picks you up and delivers you to your destination. The whole transaction is cashless, you pay Uber and Uber pays the driver. You don't need to own a car, pay for insurance and maintenance, pay for fuel, pay to park, and you don't even have to have a place to keep the car. If there are enough Uber drivers in your area, and one is available when you want to travel, you are all set. Just imagine a driverless car picking you up and delivering you to your destination. Since Uber wouldn't have to pay a human driver, the cost of a ride should be significantly lower.

As you can see, there are a number of great reasons why you might want to own, or at least support, self-driving cars. Ah, but with any technology, there could be a dark side to these autonomous vehicles as well. So, why wouldn't you want to have one of these cool, high tech cars? There are a number of concerns.

- Probably the most serious concern for most of us is how the car would react in the case of an unavoidable accident. Remember, if the car is in total control, the algorithms (programs) the car uses will have to guide it in ANY situation. Now I grant you these situations are relatively rare. Hopefully they will never happen to you. But when programming an autonomous vehicle, they must be considered. So let's look at some examples of classic problems that could face a self-driving car.

  - In an article entitled, "Why Self-Driving Cars Must Be Programmed to Kill", the authors look at 3 different scenarios.

    - The first is the case where a pedestrian walks into the roadway inside the braking distance of the car. In other words, the pedestrian steps into the street so close to the front of the moving car that it will be impossible to stop the car before hitting the pedestrian. At that point the car would have two choices, either hit the pedestrian, or veer off the roadway into a wall, possibly killing the driver. Which choice should the car make?

Should it sacrifice the pedestrian to protect the driver, or should it risk the life of the driver to save the pedestrian?

- In the second case, which is similar to the first, suppose a group of people suddenly walk into the roadway in front of the car and inside the braking distance. Again, which choice should the car make, protect the driver, or protect the pedestrians by potentially sacrificing the driver?

- The third case is somewhat like the second, but with a twist. The car has two choices, either plow into the group of pedestrians, or veer off the roadway and strike a single pedestrian. In either of these two cases, someone will most likely die.

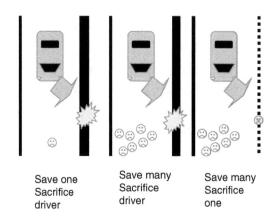

Save one
Sacrifice
driver

Save many
Sacrifice
driver

Save many
Sacrifice
one

Figure 3   Three possible scenarios...no good answer!.

- The research done on peoples' judgements in these three scenarios is fascinating. These three situations were presented to a number of people. They were asked to pick the appropriate response for the program (car.) If the people viewed these from the point of view of an anonymous person, they most often chose to have the car to minimize the loss of life. However, when the participants were asked to put themselves INTO the car, (they became the "driver,") then they were not all that keen on having the car sacrifice them to save anonymous pedestrians. There is a compounding problem. If we accept that self-driving cars will save lives in general, but the programming of those cars is such that people won't buy them, then more lives could be lost just because there are fewer self-driving cars on the roads. So, the telling question, would YOU buy a car that put the life and safety of an anonymous pedestrian over your life and safety?

- What about the situation where the autonomous car avoids hitting a motorcycle and instead veers off the roadway, putting its "driver" at risk? Is it acceptable to put the "driver" at risk if the odds of his/her surviving are better than the motorcycle rider's chance of survival?

There is another thorny problem raised by these cars. Who is liable when the car "decides" to perform an action that results in a person being harmed, or even worse, killed? Would the car manufacturer be at fault for the way the car was programmed or would the driver be held responsible because he/she owns the vehicle? And what if you had "ethics switches" that could be set to tell your car how you wanted it to react if faced with a situation where someone or even several someones lives were at risk? Would you, then, take the responsibility for the way your car chose to react? Suppose you could set your car to choose children over adults, in other words, spare the child and risk the adult. Or suppose it could be programmed to preserve the driver at all costs? Would the manufacturer be less liable if all they did was allow the driver to select parameters that chose specific values? As you can see, this is a very complex and unpleasant legal conundrum that has to be addressed before autonomous vehicles can be allowed to freely roam our streets. Now, in the case of delivery vehicles, the choice should seem to be simpler, save the people at the expense of the load. Ah, but what if the load were toxic, and the resulting crash, while saving the people directly involved, caused harm to others as a result of the spill? As you can see, questions like these are very difficult to answer! We could possibly limit the manufacturer's liability when an autonomous vehicle injures a person, much like vaccine makers are protected if their vaccines cause harm. In that case, the belief that immunizations are essential to keep the population healthy out weighs the potential harm of a few. Could that be the solution for robot cars? Time will tell...but you do need to think about it.

Another very worrisome problem that faces self-driving cars is the potential for the computers that control them to be hacked. Yup, self-driving cars are just a large number of computes all networked together. They could possibly be hacked by someone bent on mischief or worse. Suppose a hacker thought it would be great fun to limit all the cars on a given freeway at a given time to a top speed of 20 mph. That would make your commute horrible, and if you couldn't override the computer, you would be stuck in a slowly moving traffic jam with no option but to endure. But the possibilities are much darker than that. Back in 2013, a writer for Wired magazine drove a Toyota Prius and a Ford Escape with a pair of hackers in the back seat. The hackers had a laptop connected to a cable plugged into the car's diagnostic port. The hackers were able to take control of the brakes, steering, seat belt tensioning, and horn. While it was disconcerting for the writer, there was comfort in knowing that to take control of his car, the hackers had to be physically wired into the vehicle.

All that changed when auto makers began to turn their cars into mobile hot spots. According to one article, if a car is connected to the Net, anyone who can determine the car's IP (Internet Protocol) address can send commands to the car. That allows the hacker to remotely control many of the critical systems. Hackers no longer have to be physically hardwired into the car, they can control the target vehicle from anywhere they can get a network connection. And the things they can already control are frightening. Not only can they tune the radio and control its volume, they can take over the heating/cooling system, lock the doors, tension or loosen the seat belts, and enable, disable, or deploy the airbags. Those are bad enough, but these hackers also controlled the transmission, the throttle, brakes, and the steering! That's right, a hacker with the right software could take over your car, lock the doors, disable the airbags, accelerate up to the car's maximum speed, disable the brakes, and then steer the car off the road into obstacles. What if a hacker took control of a car and then used it as a weapon? And all these hacks are possible given the current level of automation. What happens when your car is merely one of a herd of autonomous vehicles driving down the freeway?

One of the main reasons autonomous vehicles are so vulnerable to hacking is that the software, and there is a lot of software, wasn't designed to handle any sort of attack. As to how much software there is, well, the Apollo 11 space ship ran about 145,000 lines of code. The Android operating system has about 12 million lines, and a modern car...over 100 million lines of code. Before cars were put on the Net, all of the integrated systems controlling the car could trust the commands they were given. There was no way one system could lie to another, or give bad commands because the car was a self-contained, isolated, secure network. But if a hacker can compromise just one system, he/she can use that system to co-opt all the other systems. So far, one of the most common ways current hackers attack is through the audio system. That code was never intended to resist attack.

Let's look at a specific example. In an article in Wired magazine in July of 2015, the author was driving a Jeep Cherokee in St. Louis. He was testing whether a pair of hackers could remotely alter the behavior of his vehicle. As he was driving down he freeway at 70 MPH, his AC system came on, at full blast, and he hadn't touched the controls. Then his radio began playing music from a local hip-hop station at full volume. When he tried to adjust the volume, or just turn off the radio nothing changed. Hackers were in control of both systems. Next the windshield washers and wipers came on, and stayed on, once again out of his control. But things got worse. Suddenly his jeep shifted into neutral, and stayed there. Pumping the gas pedal increased the engine speed, but the car didn't respond and kept coasting because the hackers were controlling the transmission. Eventually the hackers, sitting over 10 miles away, told him to exit, turn the jeep off and restart it. When he did that they gave him back control. After he exited the roadway, and was in a safe parking lot, the hackers once more took control of his jeep, but this time they disabled the brakes. The author was unable to keep his jeep from rolling into a ditch at the edge of the parking lot.

In July of 2016 BMW announced that its cars had two major vulnerabilities that would allow hackers to take over the vehicle.

So hackers can already take control of a vehicle remotely, and before autonomous cars become commonplace, this problem must be fixed. And that is a BIG problem, but there are others. For example, Google cars can't "see" smaller objects in the roadway. It's commonly called the "squirrel problem", since the Google car doesn't react to squirrels in the roadway...thump, thump....I hate when that happens!

The Volkswagen Diesel hack is another example of how the software in an existing car can be altered without the knowledge of the driver. It seems that the programmers at Volkswagen altered the code controlling the emissions system. When the car detected that it was hooked up to a testing center, all the pollution control systems worked as they were supposed to. However, once the vehicle was disconnected from the testing machine, it reverted to giving the owner better performance by doing less pollution control! That was great from a fuel saving and performance point of view, but not so good for the environment. This was a very elegant hack, in my opinion, because it gave the owner a better performing, more fuel efficient vehicle. However, it did break the rules. Disclaimer, your humble author owns, drives, and loves a little Volkswagen Golf diesel. Mine, being an older model, does not contain the emissions hack, but I am a wee bit prejudiced when it comes to that engine.

Another example of this sort of hack (on a positive note) is called "chipping" your vehicle. The main ECU can be reprogrammed to give the vehicle better acceleration, or better mileage than the default factory settings. While the vehicles will still pass emissions testing, they can be "tweaked" to better match the needs of their owner.

As I write this, in 2016, these are some of the things that autonomous cars still can't do.

- Handle bad weather. Snow, sleet, heavy rain, fog, all of these present special problems to self-driving cars. Snow and heavy rain blur or obscure lane markers. Heavy rain, dense fog, or snow will limit how far the RADAR and LiDAR can see. And on top of that when the road surface becomes slippery, the car has problems adjusting to changing road conditions.

- Go anywhere...anywhere that there isn't a detailed map that is. If your robot car can't get a network connection or at least a cell signal, at worst it will stop and wait for one. At best, it will give you control of the vehicle.

- Take direction from traffic police. While the car will be able to tell that there is a person standing in the roadway, waving his/her arms in a peculiar manner, the car won't be able to follow the officer's directions and run the stop sign, only turn left, etc.

- And, of course, small animals running across the roadway are still in grave danger.

There is a lot of discussion about these vehicles, and a lot of differing opinions as to both how and when they will be implemented. One way to look at the evolution of autonomous vehicles comes from the National Highway Traffic Safety Administration (NHTSA). They have developed a 5 step continuum to describe the implementation of self-driving cars:

Level 0: The state that most of us are in now, where the driver is in complete control of all functions of the vehicle. (This discounts things like anti-lock brakes and normal cruise control).

Level 1: One of the functions of the vehicle is automated. For example, autonomous cruise control, self parking, or lane detection. Some vehicles are now at this level, but usually it is reserved for the high end luxury market.

Level 2: More than one function is automated. For example, lane detection along with autonomous cruise control and self steering. This is the level the most advanced vehicles have reached in mid 2016. At this level, the human operator must be vigilant and always ready to intervene should the software make a mistake. An interesting example of this level of autonomy showed up on YouTube in the late summer of 2015. A Tesla S, at that time one of the most advanced autonomous cars available, operating at Level 2, decided that an oncoming car was the car it was supposed to "follow." To accomplish that the Tesla changed lanes, into the oncoming traffic lane, to "follow" that oncoming car! Only a quick response by the driver averted a head on collision!

Level 3: All the driving functions are automated enough to allow the driver to perform other tasks like reading, texting, etc. At level 3 most of the controls are obsolete. There is really no great need for steering wheels, accelerator pedals, or brakes. About all the "driver" would control are the cabin temperature and entertainment system.

Level 4: When autonomous vehicles reach this point, they will be completely outside driver control, and can operate without a human "driver" at all. When vehicles reach this level, taxi cabs, Uber cars and the like will be free to roam the streets looking for passengers. Level 4 delivery vehicles will be sharing the road, carrying their loads with no human aboard unless the human is necessary to load and/or unload the cargo.

Pretty much everyone agrees that once some of the autonomous features, especially forward collision and lane departure warning systems, blind spot assist, automatic breaking, and adaptive cruise control are implemented on all vehicles in the U.S., it will save a significant number of lives. When/if vehicles reach level 4, we will see another large reduction in lives lost as that will eliminate many of the driver errors that cause accidents. Other benefits include lower traffic congestion, and increased mobility for people who cannot drive themselves at all. Finally, research seems to show that when the entire fleet of private vehicles are autonomous fuel economy will increase and emissions will decrease just because vehicles will accelerate and brake less often.

So, what is the bottom line? It seems that while the idea of autonomous vehicles is appealing from several points of view, like lives and resources saved, there is a dark side to this technology as well. The biggest obstacle to universal adoption is the necessity for everyone to buy into and purchase autonomous vehicles. You see, if only 95% of the drivers have autonomous cars, the remaining 5% can wreak havoc on the streets. This may be a decision you will be faced with, not in the immediate future but perhaps in the next decade or so. So....would you trust the programmers with YOUR life? Please keep a close eye on the development of autonomous cars, and especially keep up to date on those sneaky black boxes! I must admit, the transition from an active, engaged, driver to baggage with no control at all is not one that I am looking forward to!

As this text is getting ready to go to the printers, several problems with Autonomous vehicles have come to light. In one incident, the driver of a Tesla was killed, and in others, Tesla's Autopilot is blamed for accidents. Please refer to the "Further Research: Tesla Accidents" below to find links to articles discussing these events.

FURTHER RESEARCH

A History of Autonomous Vehicles - Computer History Museum www. computerhistory.org/.../where-to-a-histo...

Autonomous Cars Through the Ages | WIRED www.wired.com/2012/02/ autonomous-vehicle-history/

Autonomous Cars and Society - Worcester Polytechnic ... https://www.wpi. edu/.../IQPOVP06B1.pdf

Autonomous Cars | Just another WordPress site autonomouscars.com/

PDF]Autonomous Vehicle Technology – RAND Corporation www.rand.org/ content/...1/RAND_RR443-1.pdf

http://www.pcmag.com/article2/0,2817,2493183,00.asp?mailing_ id=1480931&mailing=DailyNews&mailingID=4678F935FE99A55A8FE-0388BEF849DA2

http://www.researchgate.net/publication/221611849_Effect_of_Proactive_ Braking_on_Traffic_Flow_and_Road_Throughput

Hacking Autonomous Vehicles
http://www.wired.com/2015/07/hackers-remotely-kill-jeep-highway/
http://www.wired.com/2015/08/hackers-cut-corvettes-brakes-via-common-car-gadget/

http://thehackernews.com/2015/10/hacking-car-airbag.html

http://www.thesecurityblogger.com/zero-day-flaw-lets-hackers-tamper-with-your-car-through-bmw-portal/

LiDAR applications

http://grindgis.com/data/lidar-data-50-applications

Mystery traffic jams

http://phys.org/news/2007-12-traffic-mystery-mathematicians.html

Tesla Accidents

http://www.nytimes.com/2016/07/13/business/tesla-autopilot-fatal-crash-investigation.html?_r=0

http://www.bbc.com/news/technology-36783345

A different look:

http://www.vanityfair.com/news/2016/07/how-the-media-screwed-up-the-fatal-tesla-accident

Please search out more recent articles, I feel sure that this will become more common.

Tor (The Onion Router)

What is The Onion Router? No, it isn't something that makes you cry, nor is it a way to get onions from farm to market. Rather, it is a way to use the Internet in a relatively anonymous way. Tor wraps your precious Web traffic in a series of layers of protection, much like the layers of an onion, hence the name. Let's look at how it works.

Imagine you want to send a super-secret birthday card to your friend Emily in Fort Worth and you didn't want her, or anyone else, to know it came from you. If you mailed the card directly from your mailbox, Emily would see from the post-mark that the card came from your home town of Memphis, and since you are her only friend in Memphis, she would immediately know the card came from you. Anyone else (who knew you were Emily's friend) could figure it out, too. To prevent that you could put the original card (already in a stamped and addressed envelope) into another envelope and mail the nested envelopes to your friend Sarah in Chicago. Inside the outer envelope, along with the envelope containing your envelope to Emily, you would put instructions for Sarah to mail the inner envelope from her post office. To further confuse the trail, you could then put Sarah's letter in another envelope, with instructions, and mail it to Jared in Houston. (You could keep doing this, sending the card to more and more friends, each of them sending the card to the next person. For this illustration, two links or steps are sufficient.)

Now, when Jared mails his enclosed envelope to Sarah, and she mails the enclosed envelope to Emily, no one who sees the final envelope will have any idea that the

Figure 1 Emily's envelope is inside Sarah's envelop which is inside Jared's.

message to Emily originated from Memphis. If Emily looks at the postmark, she will see the message was mailed from Chicago, and if she tracks Sarah down, Sarah could only tell Emily that the envelope she got came postmarked from Houston. Emily would have to then figure out that Jared, in Houston, sent the envelope to Sarah, and the likelihood of that happening is slim. If you added a few more friends to the chain, it would become nigh on impossible for anyone to determine where the card had originally came from.

Now let's take it one step further. If you really wanted to keep the sending location secret, you could encrypt, or encode, the information on the original card in such a way that only Emily could decode it.–provided Emily has the key to decrypt the information). That way, if somebody steamed open the envelope(s), all they would see is gibberish, not anything that identified you in any way. That is what the Tor network does. It will encrypt all the data so that anyone looking at it will see nothing of value. Even the mighty NSA has a problem with this type of encrypted data; they can't make heads nor tails out of it either! That is what anonymity is all about—being able to keep private anything you don't wish to share with others. The only problem with this sort of mail source hiding is that it is slower than just sending Emily the card directly. Likewise, a Tor session usually returns results more slowly than you might be used to. It is, however, a small price to pay for anonymity.

Now let's get a little more technical. What really happens when you use Tor? Your information is encrypted soon as it enters the Tor network. In addition, Tor strips off some of the information like which kind of computer you have, what operating system you use, etc. Then Tor encrypts all the remaining addressing information. Once encrypted, the data, encapsulated in a *packet*, are sent sequentially to a number of different, random, servers which effectively hide the original source. In addition, since the data are all encrypted, should someone peek at the packet, all they would see is an encrypted mess. When the packet reaches the last router before its destination, that machine will decrypt information and pass it to the destination device. This brings up a very important point! If you don't use a secure Web site, one whose URL starts with HTTPS, your data will be vulnerable when in transitions to the Tor network from your browser, and from Tor network to the final destination machine. You can avoid this by only accessing sites that use secure HyperText Transport Protocol (HTTPS).

But there is an even easier way! You can also insure that the data are encrypted from your computer to the Tor network by using a Tor browser. You can get your own, personal, special copy of the Tor software package at the following website:

https://www.torproject.org/download/download-easy.html.en

I urge you to get a copy of the Tor browser, and use it regularly. It's always good to be anonymous on the Internet.

There are couple of things that you can't do in the Tor network. For example, the default Tor-enabled browser blocks Flash animations because they can be exploited or used to reveal your computer's specific IP address. Unfortunately for some of us, that includes some YouTube videos. Luckily, YouTube also serves videos using pure HTML5 for compatible browsers. You also need to be careful about opening any documents you download through the Tor network. Some of those documents may contain code that can be used to expose your home computer's address, or otherwise compromise your system. For example, if you download a music file and then play it using Windows media player, or any other music playing software that accesses the Internet to determine information about the song, that Internet access will be through your normal connection and not the Tor network, unless your machine is configured to route all outbound traffic through Tor. If some nefarious person were tracking who played that song, they could possibly identify your IP address when the media player requested information about that particular song.

Finally, for those of you who are more technologically savvy, the Tor project advises to never try to use bit torrent with Tor. Those two packages just don't play well together, due to the bandwidth requirements associated with peer-to-peer file sharing.

That is pretty much how the Tor network works. On the Internet, all data are encapsulated within data structures called a packets. The packet acts like an envelope that encloses the data and contains, in part, addressing data for both the packet's source and destination. If you send packets directly from your computer to another computer, the packets will show that they come from your computer's IP address. However, if you choose to use the Tor network, then your packets will be sent, randomly, from one IP address to another, several times, confusing the "from" address and masking the original source of the packets. In addition, throughout the Tor network your data are encrypted for additional security.

There are additional anonymity problems with the Internet. Most of the browsers and search engines keep detailed records of each search term you enter, and which pages you open (click on) following that search. They do that so they can put the search results in an order that tries to put the pages they think you will most likely want to see first in the list. That sounds pretty neat, actually, but for those of us who are concerned with anonymity and privacy, it has creepy ramifications. This "service" that is provided by the search engines has been given the not so polite name, "The Google Bubble" because it was identified early in the Google search engine.

THE GOOGLE "BUBBLE"

When discussing privacy and anonymity, it is critical to consider the phenomenon called "The Google Bubble." This is a "feature" of most of the current search engines, and is generally done using cookies, small data files, stored in the browser, which link back to database entries stored on the search engine's

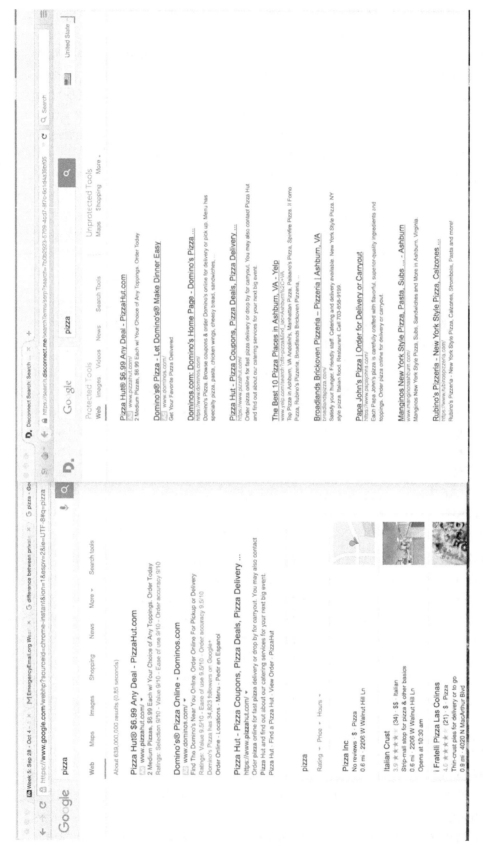

Figure 2   Google Chrome vs a TOR browser using the same search term.

database. As such, the browser plays a small role in predictive typing and search profiling. It has also been incorporated into several of the social media sites like Facebook. The initial idea was great. The algorithm was supposed to make your search results more relevant to you by screening out results that didn't match your browsing/searching history and organizing the relevant results in a useful order with the most likely data returned put first in the list...

Now, let's look closely at the results in Figure 2. Notice that the results returned in Google Chrome are all in Irving, Texas (where I was when I did the searching), but the results in the Tor browser are for Ashburn, Virginia! The search engine is still using my location, but it thinks I am in Virginia, not Texas. That shows us that:

1. Tor is, indeed, randomizing my location.

2. The search engine is trying to use my current location to filter results!

All but one of the search engines that I have used apply similar "relevant results" algorithms to try to make the order of the returned results as meaningful as possible. They do this by remembering the words you searched for before, the links you clicked on, and your current physical location. In some cases, the search engines also take into account the links other users have clicked on, especially if this is the first time you searched for that term. Using those four criteria, the search engine filters or ranks the returned links, deciding what to display first. Facebook uses the similar algorithms to decide which of your friends to push up to the top of your homepage. Some of the time this is a Good Thing, however, there are also some problems:

1. "Relevant results" can give you a false sense of what the majority of people are thinking. Before the advent of the Google Bubble, search results were returned based upon the number of times people selected a specific link.

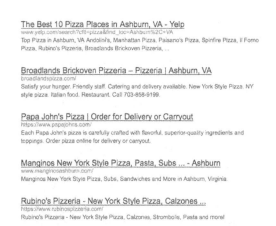

Figure 3 A randomized location from TOR *Closeup of search results, notice the LOCATON!*

That meant that the results gave a good example of what most people looked at based on a specific search term. That is no longer the case. For example, if I only click on links and/or search for pages that are Democratic, and I most often interact with my Democratic friends' posts on Facebook, Google and Facebook will begin showing me Democratic links/friends first. After a while, I could come to believe that almost everybody was of a Democratic mind set, that ALL my friends were Democrats, etc. I call these "incestuous results" because they reinforce my existing beliefs and do NOT give me a fair and balanced look at the world. Granted, when I am looking for the nearest pizza place, this is great. After all, do I really care about pizza parlors in Virginia when I am sitting in Irving, Texas? But if I don't know what the browser is doing to the results, I can be badly mislead.

2. Notice what I said above, the browsers and search engines REMEMBER the things you searched for before! That's right, somewhere in the vastness of the cloud your whole search history is neatly tucked away ready to "help" with your next search. Do you really want someone to keep all those data on your searches? In a study conducted a few years ago, one of the big search engines released several gigabytes of anonymized search data it had collected. The data were stripped of all identifying fields, and each user was assigned a random identifier. NO ID data were shared at all. None the less, it took the research team analyzing the data less than a week to identify by name and physical address some of the people whose data were used. That's right, just by looking at search terms and search frequencies, the researchers were still able to identify specific individuals. So, my question to you is: do you really want your search engines to keep track of everything you search for, and everything you click on after each search? Really?

3. Recently, researchers have identified a third possible problem associated with these filtering algorithms. They claim that search engines are behaving in racist and sexist ways. For example, if you search for a name that is uncommon among Anglos, the browser is more likely to pop up a window allowing you to run an online, criminal background check. Initially the odds of a background checking pop up appearing were random. However, if people more often clicked on the background check after searching for a non-Anglo name, then over time the search engine decreased the odds of that popup appearing when Anglo names were searched. Similarly, when people with traditionally female names searched for jobs, the algorithm usually returned lower paying jobs than when names that are usually male entered the same search string. In theory, women, mistakenly thinking they were not qualified for the higher paying jobs, didn't click on the high paying jobs as often. Over time, the search engine modified the results it returned based on the

assumed gender of the searchers name, putting the most commonly selected results first. Obviously, a computer program cannot be sexist or racist! It is just a set of instructions for the computer. Unfortunately, using the Google Bubble algorithm, the results of a search can appear to be both. Programs that use relevant result algorithms learn and modify their behavior. Let's look at an example. Emma and Eric, are personal assistants to an executive at a technological company. They would both like to change jobs. When Emma searches for professional assistant jobs, the search engine will most likely show her lower level jobs than they would show Eric, her fellow employee. Even if Emma and Eric had the exact same job description, exactly the same qualifications, exactly the same work experience, based on the way the search engine evaluates their names, it would present lower paying jobs to a female name! Yikes!!

One of the search engines that doesn't keep any records of where I am, what I have ever searched for, or what I click on is DuckDuckGo: https://duckduckgo. com/ Because this search engine keeps no data about you, or your location, or what you are searching for, or what you clicked on, your searching session will be fairly private. If you want to be doubly sure your searches are anonymous, you can use a Tor browser to access the DuckDuckGo site. Give it a try. It is a pretty fast search engine, and you can breathe easier knowing that there are no data kept about your searching session.

"Ah", you exclaim, "but I am not doing anything illegal, I am not a Bad Guy, so why do I care?" Good question! Let's look at the interesting tale of the Catalano family. It seems that Mr. Catalano's backpack had torn, so he needed a new backpack. He was looking for good deals on the Net from his office computer upstairs in his home. Later that same day, his wife was looking for a replacement pressure cooker since theirs was beginning to leak. Now, you need to understand that this happened in late 2013, the same year that the Boston marathon terrorists used pressure cookers to make bombs, and concealed those bombs in backpacks. Nonetheless, shortly after the couple, unbeknownst to each other, searched for those two incriminating phrases, six members of a Terrorism Taskforce forcibly entered their home, searched it top to bottom. They spent several hours asking Mr. Catalano numerous questions about his and his wife's backgrounds, employment, political views, and their intent in doing those searches. Fortunately for her, his wife happened to be away from the house. After a while the officers left, and neither of the Catalanos were jailed. However, their privacy was invaded, all because of a couple of search terms that came from their home Internet Protocol address. Let's suppose, just for discussion, that the authorities had found something damaging in the Catalano's house. For example, suppose Mrs. Catalano was a competitive pistol shooter and reloaded her own ammunition. Then the search would have turned up a quantity of smokeless gun powder! It's totally legal to own gun powder, it's totally legal to search for backpacks and pressure cookers, but the outcome of that search could have been vastly different even though no one broke any laws! And all that was triggered by a couple of innocent searches. Now, I must ask again, do you really want your search engines keeping track of everything you search for, and everything you click on after each search?

But what about the other side of the coin? What if some bad dude, some seriously bad person uses this type of communications to research, plan, and coordinate some horrific act? That is, indeed, a possibility. This is one of the great questions of our time. Before you answer the question, you need to remember a few things:

First, technology, by its very nature, is neutral. A scalpel, as technology, is neither good nor bad. What matters is how it is being used. If it is used to save the life of a critically injured patient, it is good use of that technology. If the very same scalpel is used to rob or harm somebody, it is a bad use of that same technology.

Second, when people use this argument with me, my question for them is: "So you would be comfortable with Web cameras that you can't control watching you in your bathroom, and in your bedroom, at all times, right?" Of course they balk at this, saying something like, "Well, of course NOT, I have a right to privacy!" And I whole heartedly agree. In the same way, you have a right to privacy in your own home, you have an absolute right to privacy in your digital communications and your digital searches. In fact, you have an absolute right to your privacy all across your digital life!

Third, we need to remember one of the sayings of Benjamin Franklin: "Those who would give up essential liberty, to purchase a little temporary safety, deserve neither liberty nor safety." You have the essential liberty of free speech, and nowhere does it say that that speech cannot be encrypted or not recorded. If we, collectively, give up our right or liberty to be secure in our speech, then our speech is no longer free. Yes, private, secure browsing may be used for evil, but it can also be used for good. Suppose you are a young girl, and you notice that your body is changing as you mature. If your parents were not willing or able to discuss those changes with you, wouldn't it be valuable if you could do anonymous Internet searches to try to see what is happening to you? Suppose you live in a repressive society where just searching for the term "America" could result in your being arrested or worse. Wouldn't it be worth a lot to be able to search anonymously if you were curious? I could continue to list example after example, but I am sure you can think of better examples, closer to your own life. Privacy and anonymity are becoming two of the absolutely critical questions of our time, yet we will have to address this fundamental problem over and over again. But we must look at the big picture, not an isolated case, when we make decisions that involve the loss of essential liberties.

Fourth, again we go to Franklin: "That it is better 100 guilty persons should escape than that one innocent person should suffer." And Franklin is not the only one to voice this belief. Voltaire said, "that 'tis much more Prudence to acquit two Persons, tho' actually guilty, than to pass Sentence of Condemnation on one that is virtuous and innocent." And the famous legal scholar and judge, Sir William Blackstone, echoed this when he said, "For the law holds, that it is better than ten guilty persons escape, than that one innocent suffer." So, which is better: a system that tracks your activity and attempts to infer your intentions (violating your privacy, like the Catalanos case), or one where data can be exchanged anonymously (even if the occasional criminal gets away with a crime) so that the vast majority of innocents are protected from wrongful accusation and privacy violations? I leave it to you to contemplate that last question, and hope as you do, that you will think long and hard about the potential costs and benefits of each choice.

As this book was going to print, some technical problems were identified with the Tor network.

https://www.deepdotweb.com/2016/05/09/tor-viable-alternative/

Ransomware (The New and growing threat)

If you still need a reason to back up the programs and data on your computer at regular (preferably short), intervals, let's hope this section will provide that reason! *Ransomware* is a type of malware that performs a specific and terrible function. According to Symantec, a digital security company, ransomware is the most troublesome type of malware of our time. When ransomware infects your computer, the malware will encrypt some or all of your files, and/or may lock you out of your computer. To get your system back and/or restore your data, you will have to pay the ransomware owner, (data-napper?) a fee, or ransom. Then they will, sometimes, send you the key unlock your system or decrypt your data. Unfortunately, there is NO guarantee that the key they send you will actually decrypt your data. In most cases the ransomer will request payment in Bitcoin because that is almost always untraceable. In some cases the victim is only given a short window of time to reply with payment, after which time the hacker deletes the key. Without the key, the victim's system can never be recovered, and will need to be completely wiped clean, all the programs reloaded, and all his data will need to be either restored or recreated. On the other hand, a wise computer user routinely backs up his system, so all he would have to do is restore his system to the day, or hour, before he was attacked from his backups. Of course, he would then need to avoid opening the attachment, running the program, or looking at the image that infected his computer!

HISTORY

The first "official" ransomware program, called "AIDS Trojan" also known as the PC Cyborg Virus, was developed in 1989 by biologist Joseph Popp. He loaded the virus onto 20,000 floppy disks labeled "AIDS Information – Introductory Diskettes." He distributed these floppy disks to attendees of the 1989 World Health Organization conference on AIDS. This was a very patient virus, which waited until the infected computer had been booted or re-booted 90 times, at which point the software would activate. It would hide all directories, and encrypt the names of all the files on the C: or the main disk drive. To regain access to the files, the user would have to send $189 to the PC Cyborg Corp. via a Panama post office box. Since this malware was only delivered via an infected floppy disk, the spread was limited. The encryption was also fairly easy to break, so while this particular malware had little effect on the world of computing, it was the harbinger of things to come.

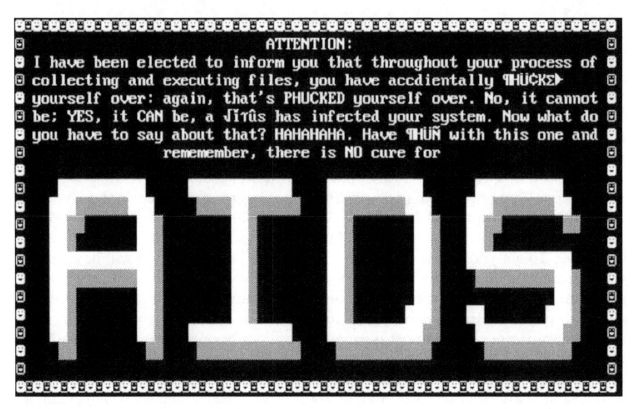

Figure 1   A screen shot of the image the user of a computer infected with the AIDS Trojan (Pardon the language).

2005

The first incidences of true ransomware infection happened in Russia in late 2005. In those attacks, the malware selected specific files, and *zipped* them into a password protected compressed file. Next it replaced the original instances of the programs or files with these compressed and encrypted versions. Finally, the ransomware prompted the victim to pay for the password to the encrypted files. In this case, the files selected were mostly .doc, .xls, .exe, and .dll files. Obviously, these files are critical to the function of the computer. Other variants of this form of attack infected and modified the MBR (Master Boot Record). By infecting and modifying the MBR, the ransomware was sure to stay in place until the computer was completely wiped, or the victim paid the ransom of $300. In the successive years, this type of ransomware was mostly confined to Russia, but it did spread to some parts of Europe.

2006

In 2006, ransomware attacks moved outside Russia into the rest of Europe and the U.S. As more and more attackers began using this novel concept, new and exciting variants began to emerge. In the early days of ransomware attacks the software was most often developed by amateur programmers so the infection rate was low. However in 2006, professional programmers and organizations moved into this arena. The Archiveus Trojan encrypted all of the documents in the victims "My Documents" folder. To receive the 30-digit password, the victim had to purchase specific items from an online pharmacy. That same year, the Gpcode Trojan was the first program to use the RSA encryption to encrypt users' data. Another type of ransomware also reared its ugly head around this time. WinLock malware locked up the user's computer and demanded that they send a $10 premium-rate SMS message to get the code to unlock their computer.

For the next several years criminals continued to evolve these two types of ransomware, and began to use a third type of pseudo-ransomware called, *"scareware."* In one variant of this attack, the malware displays a message on the user's screen telling him that his computer is infected. It then directs the user to purchase and download a special antiviral package (from the ransomer, of course), to clean up his computer. Another variant of scareware, is called police ransomware. This malware pops up a message telling the user that their computer has been used to commit some sort of crime like distributing child pornography or illegally downloading movies. To avoid prosecution, the software requires the victim to pay a fee or fine to the ransomer. Figure 2 shows an example of a scareware screen that would be shown to a US user. Users in other countries would see a screen appropriate to their own countries law enforcement authority. Notice that the only way the user has to pay the "fine" is to use "MoneyPak," an untraceable, anonymous, currency transfer program.

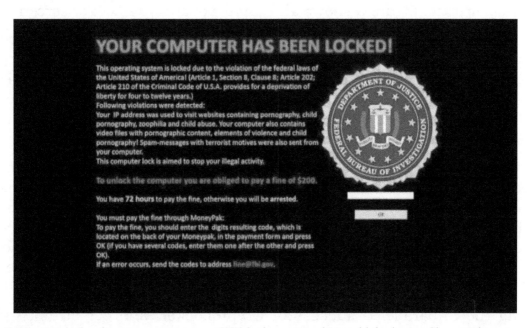

Figure 2   An example of a scareware screen (FBI lock screen: https://cbsdenver.files.wordpress.com/2012/09/computer-lock-screen.jpg).

2012

2012 was a banner year for ransomware. Professional criminal organizations discovered that there was a LOT of money to be made with this sort of software, and the variants proliferated. There were also many new versions of scareware, some using audio recordings and video files to "prove" that the infected computer had been used in the commission of a crime. But the best was yet to come.

2013

In September of 2013, a new and much more powerful form of ransomware appeared. CryptoLocker not only locked up the user's computer, it also encrypted some or all of the files on the user's hard drive using very powerful 256-bit RSA encryption. With this type of encryption, the key used to encrypt the data and the key used to decrypt the data are different. This is one of the most widely used encryption methods today. It is used as a step to secure web pages like banking, eBay, etc. To be more exact, web browsers use RSA for signatures in certificates, and to establish a secure mechanism of transmitting a symmetrical key. This symmetrical key (usually an AES key) is used for the actual encryption of webpages. AES encryption is so strong that it would take the NSA months if not years to break it. Obviously that makes it impossible for the regular user to break. Not only will the ransomer demand payment for the key to decrypt the hard drive, they demand payment be made in a very short timeframe, usually just a few days. If the payment is not made, the ransomer states she will delete the key from her server. Should that happen, the victim's hard drive can never be decrypted. Some later variants will give the victim a second chance to purchase the key at a significantly higher price. Figure 3 shows an example of a CryptoLocker screen.

One of the unique things about CryptoLocker is the strength of the encryption algorithm it uses. It would even be difficult for the NSA to break this encryption in any reasonable amount of time. Another interesting thing is that CryptoLocker accepts payment only in Bitcoin. Since that virtual money is nearly untraceable, the ransomer can take her payment and not leave any trace of where, or to whom, the money was sent.

In the first variants of CryptoLocker, the key was actually stored on the infected computer, and white hat hackers fairly quickly posted a method of finding that key and using it to decrypt all the files without having to pay the ransom. The CryptoLocker coders quickly fixed that bug, and now the decryption keys are all stored on a secure server. A team comprised of the FBI and several private industry companies were able to compromise this server, and later created an online database of private keys that allowed anyone affected to decrypt their hard drive for free.

Following the unparalleled success of CryptoLocker, another strain, Crypto-Locker 2, appeared in 2015. Due to significant differences between the two

Figure 3 An example of a later CryptoLocker notification screen (Cryptolocker screen: http://www.web-root.com/blog/wp-content/uploads/2014/05/cryptolocker1.png).

strains (including the language they were written in), computer security experts believe they were created by different developers. In early 2016, the ransomware universe took an even more serious turn for the worse. A series of *exploit kits* became available that allowed criminals to use a set of pre-packaged malicious web pages to deliver ransomware to the unsuspecting user. Not only were these exploit kits available for sale, but the nefarious criminal could lease both the delivery system and a strong variant of CryptoLocker. The owner of the exploit kit would agree to let a crook use the software, and deliver the CryptoLocker code, for a percentage of the money that CryptoLocker generated! So if you wanted to get into the ransomware business, you could buy or license a complete tool kit to get you started! Security experts are expecting the number of ransomware attacks to steadily increase as more and more exploit kits become available.

UPDATE: The summer of 2016 has seen ransomware attacks multiply like rabbits. This has become the number one security problem for many, many companies. Ransomware is alive and well and coming to a computer near you!

The rise in ransomware has eclipsed other forms of cyber attacks. Criminals discovered that stealing credit card data was tedious, time intensive, and had a much lower return on investment than ransomware, due in part to many of the stolen cards already being close to their maximum limits. We can expect more powerful malware to appear as the security folks find ways to protect against the current generation. This is a constant battle; the bad guys develop an attack, the good guys find a defense, so the bad guys enhance their attack, etc. Round and round it goes.

There is also the problem of poorly written code. In November of 2015, a variant of CryptoLocker appeared on the Net. Unfortunately, the writer, a novice, altered the way the RSA keys are generated. The problem is, the code ended up irreversibly encrypting the user's data. The key it generates will be invalid. If you are so unfortunate as to become infected with this variant, called Power Worm, there is no way you can decrypt your files. The author requests a ransom of 2 Bitcoin, but even if you pay the ransom, your files will remain encrypted. There is only one way to recover your files if you have been infected by Power Worm ... restore your files from your recent backup!

So how do you protect yourself from a ransomware infection? Actually, there are three ways:

1. Disconnect your computer from the Internet, forever. That way there is no way you can become infected by an exploit-kit-created web page. Just hope you haven't already been infected when you disconnect.
2. Put aside some money to pay off the data-nappers and hope they give you a working key to decrypt your system.
3. Backup your files often, really often! Don't end up like Methodist Hospital in Kentucky or Presbyterian Medical Center in Hollywood. Both hospitals were infected with ransomware, and both ended up paying off the criminals to get their patient databases decrypted. Presbyterian Medical Center paid 40 Bitcoin (about $17,000) for the key to their patient data files. Not only were the hospitals data files at risk, but many critical services like CT scans, lab work, and even the pharmacy were shut down because those services depended on the patient files. Neither hospital had backed up their data recently, and so were vulnerable to a ransomware attack. Also, don't have the problem that several of the United States federal government had. From June, 2015 until the end of March, 2016 the U.S. federal government was the victim of over 320 ransomware attacks. Most were attacks against individual workstations. Those attacks were just part of the problem, however. Since 2005, according to the FBI Internet Complaint Center over 7,690 reports of ransomeware attacks that have been perpetrated against US citizens and companies. These attacks garnered the ransomers over $57.6 million!

You do make backups often, now don't you?! That's right, back up early and often! The data you save may be your own! :)

GLOSSARY

Term	Definition
Exploit kit	This is a very nice little package that includes everything necessary to successfully launch a ransomware attack or exploit. Depending upon the preferred method of attack, it can contain a complete web page that will infect any user who browses the page, or a set of files to be emailed to the victim. Using an exploit kit practically any user can become a crypto-criminal since deploying this collection of files requires little or no expertise.
Ransomware	A specialized type of malware that either takes over the computer's video output, or, more commonly, encrypts some or all of the files on the user's hard disk drive, or both! If the user pays a fee, the author of the ransomware may send the user a key which might unlock the encrypted files. However, this option is not always available.
Scareware	A specific type of ransomware that doesn't encrypt anything, but rather puts a message on the victim's screen telling them they have committed a crime, or that their computer has been infected with a terrible virus. This software usually locks the user's operating system until they pay either a fine for their crime, or for "special" software that will remove the horrible virus. One example of scareware is a popup that appears telling the user that they have accessed some forbidden content, often child pornography, and that they will be reported to the FBI unless they pay the virus owner a fee to ensure their silence. This could actually be called blackmailware. :)
Zipped	This is a term used to describe file(s) that have been compressed using PKZIP or another similar algorithm. Compressing, or zipping, files is a common way to reduce the space that a file takes up on disk or to make a file or files small enough to email. Zipping also allows multiple files and folders to be combined into a single file.

RESOURCES

http://www.symantec.com/content/en/us/enterprise/media/security_response/whitepapers/the-evolution-of-ransomware.pdf

https://fcw.com/articles/2016/03/30/ransomware-carper-hsgac.aspx

Money (Cash - electronic - virtual/crypto)

What is this stuff we call "Money"? Why do we have money, where did it come from and where is it going? So many questions. Let's get started answering them.

First and foremost, what is money? Basically, it started out as any medium of exchange with an agreed upon value. For example, in some societies salt, furs, or shells all were used as a medium of exchange. People have been using something to represent value for over 3000 years. There is no simple answer, but one idea that seems popular is that money was invented to act as a representative or symbol for some unit of physical work. For example, pre-money suppose I grew potatoes, and you raised chickens, and your brother had milk cows. If I wanted some milk, I would negotiate with your brother to trade some of my potatoes for some of his milk. But suppose your brother had all the potatoes he wanted? Well then, I would need to discover what he wanted, let's say eggs, and then trade my potatoes for some of your eggs, if you wanted them, Then I would have to take the eggs I received from you to your brother and trade with him for some milk. Finally I could eat my breakfast cereal! As our social group got larger, and there were more people doing specialized jobs, (yes, growing potatoes is a specialized job!) this system of trade or barter became more and more cumbersome. It might take me 4 or 5 or even more trades before I got something your brother wanted, and that is a long time to wait for breakfast!

To make life simpler, suppose we all agreed that a specific sea shell, say a cowrie shell, was worth 15 minutes of work and we agreed on how much work it took to produce a specific item. If I averaged 30 minutes planting, tending, and harvesting each potato, then I could exchange my 10 potatoes for 20 shells. If your brother's milk was valued at 4 cowrie shells per quart, (It took him an hour of work, all told, to produce a quart of milk), then I could give him 4 of my shells, take a quart of milk home, and have my breakfast. That is a LOT simpler than having to go to several people and make several trades. (Do you get the idea that I am writing this in the morning...before breakfast? 😄)

The history of how money came to be, and how different countries began by using physically available items to represent value (work) is fascinating. Even more interesting is how the idea of money, debt, credit, all the things we take for granted evolved over time. Should you want to delve more deeply into this topic, there are some resources at the end of this section. For our purposes, let's just keep it simple and say the originally money represented a unit of human work. Money or currency was crafted from an easily recognized metal like gold or silver. Each unit of the currency could be traded for a specific amount of this precious material. As an example, US currency was first based on gold, and a paper bill could be exchanged for a like value of the metal. Then the US changed over to the silver standard, and currency was based upon the value of that metal. Years ago you could take

Figure M.1   A pretty cowrie shell.

©Pavolva Elena/Shutterstock.com

a silver certificate (as the bills were known) to your bank and walk out with a lump of the metal! Coins at that time were actually made from precious metals, commonly coper, nickle, silver, rarely gold. Those coins had actual, intrinsic value. Alas, that isn't the way it is any more. In 1971 the United States ceased allowing our paper currency to be exchanged for gold. Now we have what is known as *fiat money* or fiat currency. It is no longer based upon the value of a substance it represents, and currency that cannot be redeemed for anything, but instead, currency based simply on faith in the government that issued it. And sometimes that takes a lot of faith! The term fiat means decree or pronouncement, so our money has value because the government said it does.

The history of the evolution of money, currency, is a very interesting study. For our purposes here, we will be looking at currency in a very simplistic way, it is a way to quantify and represent a unit of a person's work, represented by something that has intrinsic value like gold. Granted, with fiat currency, that is no longer strictly true, but to keep things less complex, that will be our working definition. Now let's look at what has happened in the last few decades.

First came credit cards. The money they represent is stored electronically and is hardly ever converted to any form of currency. Credit has been used since the 1800s. The early accounts were with a particular store. You ran a "tab" that was usually due at the end of the month. In the early 1900s, some oil companies issued a type of credit program for purchases with their company, but again it was limited to one merchant. In 1946, John Biggs issued a card that his customers could use to buy things at local merchants, but you had to be a customer of Biggs' bank. Of course, those cards only worked locally with merchants with which Biggs had arrangements. The first real credit card, Diners Club, was launched by Frank McNamarah in 1946. That card was limited to dining and entertainment purchases, but was the first generally available credit card. It wasn't until 1966 that Bank of America issued the first true credit card that could be used pretty much across the board. That was possible because that year most of the credit issuing banks joined into a consortium to support the use of those cards. And things got totally crazy after that. The bottom line, since the mid 1960s, some of your "money" has been, really, just a bunch of bits on someones computer somewhere. It is, for all practical purposes, *electronic currency.*

The next step in the process was debit cards. The difference between a debit card and a credit card is that the user has to have money in an account in a bank to use a debit card. Debit cards are like electronic checks. When you swipe your debit card, money, in the form of bits, is withdrawn from your account and deposited in the merchant's account just as if you had written a check to the merchant...but it happens much more quickly. Some debit cards can be set up so that they will not work if your bank account doesn't have sufficient funds to cover the transaction, others will allow you to over draft your account.

Finally, we arrive at true electronic currency. While I am not fixated on breakfast, really, I'm not, Starbucks is a good example of electronic currency. With the Starbucks application on your smart phone, you can move money from your bank account to your Starbucks "card." Then when you go to Starbucks, all you need to do to pay for your coffee and scone is let the cashier scan your smart phone's screen. Money will be deducted from the balance on your card, and transferred to Starbucks' account. It's something like a debit card, but you can't overdraw your Starbucks account. No hard currency changes hands. No one needs to figure out how to make change. You don't need to pull out your wallet. Everything is done from computer to computer...bits are exchanged.

The most important thing to remember about electronic currency is that it is simply a machine representation of actual currency. It is a simple way to handle the exchange of currency. It's still good old cowrie shells, just stored and exchanged using bits on computers instead of great, whopping bags of shells. It's a whole lot easier to lug around, too!

Our whole commerce system has come to rely on financial institutions who act as a trusted third party to any transaction. It is the financial institutions who validate the exchange of currencies, and who guarantee their worth. Electronic commerce, including Net commerce, is dependent upon these financial institutions as well. And that brings with it some problems. For example, there is a cost associated with a financial institution handling the exchange. There are no completely non-reversible transactions, because the financial institution can and will mediate between the parties in the transaction. For example, I could buy something on eBay, and then complain that the item received wasn't what I ordered. In that case, eBay could refund my purchase price, taking the money back from the seller. In this case eBay is acting as the trusted third party. Now, it is it is true that it is possible to engage in a financial transaction that seems to be exempt from the costs of the trusted third party, by using cash. However, any transaction that must be completed over the Net must use this trust based third party system. This brings us to the idea of virtual currencies.

What we need is a peer-to-peer electronic payment system that doesn't rely on the trusted third party. If the exchange was based on strongly encrypted data and was difficult if not impossible to computationally reverse, then that system would eliminate the need for the third parties. Enter the realm of *cryptocurrency*, and for our first example we will look at the most common and widely accepted medium, Bitcoin.

So what is *virtual currency* or digital currency or cryptocurrency? The best way to look at this is a collection of transaction data and digital signatures and the events associated with those transactions. Each time the owner of a cryptocurrency "spends" some, he/she signs the transfer document detailing where that particular currency is to go. Each transaction is time stamped. This transaction is then made public so anyone can verify that this particular "coin" was transferred, at a specific point in time, from person A to person B. Anyone who wishes can verify that that specific "coin" had not been transferred earlier from the same owner to another recipient. That prevents the problem of double-spending. However, to make sure of this, the entire history of each coin must be available. That history of the events involving a particular coin is called the "block-chain". Please understand that this is a simplified version of the way Bitcoin works, but it gives you the general idea. Instead of having a third party verify each transaction, people processing the math involved in the block-chain for a specific coin insure that that coin is spent only one time by a specific owner.

These digital currencies are more frequently referred to as cryptocurrency because at every step in the process of creating, storing, transferring, and spending them, all the data transmitted are very strongly encrypted.

The Bitcoins most of us use are completely virtual or digital. The vast majority of them never have a physical representation. You spend a Bitcoin, or part of a Bitcoin by transferring your Bitcoin from your digital wallet to the digital wallet of the recipient. Each transaction is entered into a public document called a *block chain*. That block chain is then reviewed and verified by any of the members of the community who wish to create, or mine, new Bitcoins. As the block chain gets longer, it takes more CPU cycles to verify it. That means that Bitcoins, and other cryptocurrency, represent units of computer work, just like physical currency represents human work. The process of verifying the block chain ensures that any Bitcoin transaction represents a true, single, instance of transfer for a specific Bitcoin. It prevents the problem of "double spending" where I use my Bitcoin to pay for something on eBay, and try to use the same Bitcoin to buy something at Starbucks. Again, Bitcoin miners perform this verification service. Since these miners invest their CPU cycles, and the electricity necessary to power their computers they need to be compensated for their time, by being paid in Bitcoins. For now, that is pretty much all you need to know to get an overview of the Bitcoin system. If you want a more detailed discussion, I will refer you to the references at the end of this section.

So to generate, or mine, your very own Bitcoin you need to use a computer to mathematically process a large block-chain, verifying that all the transactions are correct and there is no double-spending. But the problem is, you have to be the first to verify a specific part of the block-chain. As I write this, the odds for mining a Bitcoin are just a wee bit better than the odds of winning the lottery. The best way to get into Bitcoin mining is to join a pool. That means you will be working with a number of people, all using very high powered computers, and all working together to mine the block-chain. Each day the pool could mine one or more coins, and you would be rewarded a percentage of the coins mined. Your percentage is based upon how much of the actual "work" that your computer contributed to verifying the block-chain. According to the research, if you "solo-mine", you will generally mine one Bitcoin every 20+ years! And that assumes you have a relatively fast processor. If you go out and purchase a uber fast computer, you might do a bit better than that, but solo mining is usually a mistake.

I realize that this whole idea is a wee bit complex. I have simplified it here since you don't really need to know the intricacies of the Bitcoin model. However, if you feel so inclined, there are a couple of papers referenced at the end of this section that give a much more detailed explanation of just exactly how this process works.

While virtual currency is not intended to be represented by any physical object, some mints have struck actual coins that have the value of a whole, or part, of a Bitcoin. One elegant example is the Titan Bitcoin. The Titan Mint strikes a limited number of physical Bitcoins each year. The example shown here is not only a Bitcoin, it is also one Troy ounce of 99% pure gold! That means that this coin has three distinct values! The first two are different monetary values. One monetary value is the current monetary value of the Bitcoin it represents. That Bitcoin is identified using a special code hidden beneath the hologram on the back of the coin. The other monetary value is the current worth of one ounce of gold bullion. The third value is the collectable value of the physical coin, whether the hologram on the back has been removed or not. The first and last of these values are based entirely upon supply and demand. How much the Bitcoin is worth at the moment of transfer, and how much collectors are willing to pay for this particular Bitcoin. Of course, the value of the coin as bullion is fixed by the world market. Currently, an ounce of gold is worth about $1,082.

Illustration M.1   The Titan Bitcoin (Need permission to use this).

To "spend" the Titan Bitcoin, you first write down the ID number of the coin. Next you remove the hologram to expose the redemption code. Then you enter the following data into a special Website like, https://www.titanbtc.com/redeem/. On that site you will be asked for the redemption code, the coin ID, the email address associated with the coin, the password for the email address, and finally the address of the digital wallet where you want the Bitcoin transferred to. Once all those steps are completed, your physical Bitcoin becomes a collectable coin, with a value set by the market for collectable coins, and a pretty ounce of gold. As gold, it retains its bullion value, which is usually less than its collectable value. However, once you "spend" that physical Bitcoin, it loses any crypto/virtual/digital value.

To review, Bitcoin transactions are verified by folks called miners, who process the whole block-chain for a specific coin, and are rewarded in Bitcoins for their efforts. Essentially, to "mine" a Bitcoin you use your computer to run a whole bunch of complex mathematical operations on the block-chain you were given verifying that the transaction is valid. While that is pretty cool, it is also a huge amount of computing that doesn't accomplish any real, valuable work as far as the world outside the Bitcoin universe is concerned. What if there were another way to generate cryptocurrency?

Let's take a look at another cryptocurrency called CureCoin. Suppose that instead of earning coins by mathematically processing large, complex block-chains, you could be rewarded for spending your computer processing power furthering medical research? Suppose your electricity could be spent helping to find a cure for one of several terrible diseases like Alzheimers, Cancer, Huntingtons, viral diseases, and even pharmaceutical research. This is a generalized view of the process, but it will give you an idea of what you could be part of.

So, to start your very own, personal CureCoin mine all you have to do is:

1. Go to the folding at home Website and download the folding software for your particular hardware configuration. (https://folding.stanford.edu/)

2. Once you have the software installed, your computer will ask the Stanford server to send you a Work Unit (WU) and your computer will download one piece of data to be analyzed.

3. Your CPU or GPU (Graphics Processing Unit), will run the simulation software that attempts to emulate the movement of the all the atoms in a particular protein over a very short time period. Usually a nanosecond or two. There will be thousands of CPU/GPUs across the world working in tandem, trying to find a configuration for that protein. Each of them will work on one tiny increment of time. At the end of the processing, the folded protein is evaluated for potential benefits treating one or more of the diseases listed.

4. When your computer finishes processing that particular Work Unit, it will upload the results, give you credit for the work done, and ask for the next WU. All of this happens automatically, and all you have to do is sit back and collect the CureCoins. :)

5. If you don't have a fast computer, and/or you don't have a high end graphics card, you can still participate. In the Chrome browser, you can download the Google Native CLient (http://folding.stanford.edu/nacl/), and do folding in your browser. If you want to join a group, and I strongly advise you to do so, you can set up an identity and then join one of the folding groups. If you join a group, then the number of coins earned by the group as a whole is divided among the group members based upon how many Work Units each contributed to the whole.

6. To collect and hold the coins you receive, you will need a digital wallet. Before you jump into the wild and wonderful world of cryptocurrencies, I suggest you check out the Website, https://bitcoin.org/en/choose-your-wallet. You will want to follow the links on that page to insure that your coins are safe, and that your privacy is protected.

So to summarize this section, originally money was developed to allow for the exchange of goods and services where the currency represented one or more units of human work. In the beginning currency had intrinsic value. It was made of shell, or gold or silver. Over time currencies evolved away from having intrinsic value and became fiat currency. Electronic currency is nothing more than using a computer to represent some amount of real currency. Cryptocurrency is a completely different system, one that provides security and anonymity. Cryptocurrency represents machine/computer work instead of human work. The value of a cryptocurrency is dependent upon the ratio of supply and demand at the time the currency is used. This new form of money is becoming more and more popular. A number of both large and small retailers now accept cryptocurrencies in exchange for goods. For example, you can use Bitcoins with PayPal and to buy Dell computers. The list of companies is growing every day. In addition, many of the services you find on the Dark Net also accept Bitcoin. The ransomware programs expect payment in Bitcoins, and even some kidnappers are asking for ransom payments in Bitcoin. This new currency is slowly evolving into the preferred medium of exchange for anyone who values their privacy, and who wants to make an absolutely secure transfer of wealth.

RESOURCES

http://www.telegraph.co.uk/finance/businessclub/money/11174013/The-history-of-money-from-barter-to-bitcoin.html

Bitcoin image: http://www.coinworld.com/news/paper-money/2014/07/Bitcoin-coin-world-virtual-currency-titan-bitcoin-casascius-physical-bitcoin-numismatics-coin-collecting.html#

BITCOIN REFERENCES

https://bitcoin.org/en/bitcoin-paper

http://www.wired.com/insights/2015/01/block-chain-2-0/

http://www.forbes.com/sites/kellyphillipserb/2013/11/30/from-treasure-to-trash-man-tosses-out-bitcoin-wallet-on-hard-drive-worth-9-million/

GLOSSARY

Term	Definition
Block Chain	In simple terms, a block chain is a recording of every transaction made using cryptocurrency. The block-chain is a public document available to anyone for verification. Some folks, called "miners", run specialized software to verify or validate each transaction, ensuring that any given Bitcoin is only used in one transaction by a given person. These miners provide the security to the Bitcoin process and for doing that work, they are rewarded with Bitcoins. These coins represent CPU cycles used to process the block-chain (computer work), and the electricity consumed by the processing.
Cowrie Shell	The true Money Cowrie is Cypraea Monea. It lives in the Indo-Pacific tropical oceans. It is a shallow water snail that feeds on algae. The shells of this specific cowrie were used for thousands of years as a medium of exchange in Africa, Asia, and the Pacific Islands until the late 1800s.
Cryptocurrency	A form of electronic currency that is protected from counterfeiting by a strong encryption algorithm. Most of the common digital currencies in circulation are more properly called cryptocurrencies. Bitcoin, for example, is currently one of the most widely recognized cryptocurrencies on the Net. One huge advantage of using cryptocurrencies is the ease with which they can be moved from one computer to another, without the kind of expensive overhead charged by banks and other financial institutions. Another advantage of cryptocurrencies is that their use is completely anonymous. There is no way to track where a cryptocurrency came from, nor where its going. However, as there is no central repository for cryptocurrencies, if your Bitcoin wallet is stored on the hard disk of your computer, and that drive crashes, the coins that were in your wallet will be irrevocably lost. Of course that wouldn't happen to you, since you would have backed up your hard drive!! The lack of this central repository is the biggest drawback to these currencies. Back in November of 2013, a man named James Howells accidentally threw away a hard disk containing 7500 Bitcoins! He was cleaning up his computer, and that hard disk was slow, so he replaced it and threw the old drive in the trash. Today Bitcoins are trading at $329/coin, so Mr. Howells threw away a bit less than two and a half million dollars worth of Bitcoins. Those coins can never be recovered. They are lost forever!

Term	Definition
Digital Currency	See "electronic currency"
Electronic Currency	Money, stored on a digital device, and usually not converted to "hard cash". We have been using electronic currency for a long time now. When you have your paycheck "electronically deposited" in your bank account, no actual currency ever changes hands. Your employer simply instructs his or her bank to move some bits from the company account to your account. There is no hard currency involved at all. While the amount of cash on hand varies from bank to bank, and from day to day, the average bank has about $20,000 on hand, in the vault and in the ATM each day. If all the bank's customers came in at once and wanted hard currency equal to their account balance, a bank would quickly run out of cash.
Fiat Currency	This is currency that a government has declared to be legal tender, but not backed by anything physical like gold or silver. The value of this type of currency is based upon the relationship between supply and demand. It is something like an IOU. The term "fiat" comes from the latin word for decree, actually, "Let it be" so a fiat currency is one based upon faith in the government that decreed it to be legal tender. Since the value is determined by supply and demand, a government can lower the value simply by creating more of the currency. That is called inflation.
Virtual Currency	This is a form of exchange based upon the work done by a computer instead of a person. Virtual currency usually has no physical representation. One exception is the Titan Bitcoin, it is a physical coin, (the higher denominations are struck from precious metals). The way to spend this coin is to peel off the hologram on the back, leaving the coin as a collectable, physical object. Other names include "digital currency" and "cryptocurrency".

Choices (You don't always have to buy proprietary software)

Most students, unless they are exceptionally lucky, believe that there is only one reliable office suite available to them: Microsoft Office. Most people aren't even aware of the other choices! This section aims to introduce you to the popular alternatives available for Microsoft's Office products. I am not going to go into detail about Microsoft Office, your other textbooks certainly cover it. Instead, I would like to show you two (2) powerful word processing, spreadsheet, and presentation options. The first one we will look at is LibreOffice.

LibreOffice

This is the most recent iteration of OpenOffice, which was the *open source* version of the-out-of-development StarOffice. In the late 1990s, the German company Star Corp. brought out an office suite to compete with Microsoft Office in the European market. Sun Microsystems learned of this product, and bought Star Corp. They then released OpenOffice as the original open source version of StarOffice. When Sun Microsystems was acquired by Oracle, the main developers of OpenOffice left and formed The Open Document Foundation. They released LibreOffice as the most current version of this *software suite*. So, what does this term "open source" really mean?

Let's look at the process a program goes through from appearing in the imagination of the programmer, through the whole coding process, to finally end up as an executable program you can install and run on your computer.

Step 1: **Imagination:** If you can think of all the steps in a process, then you can probably create a computer program to follow that process. This is the essential first step in the design and development of any computer program, be it a game, an application, or even an operating system.

Step 2: **Design:** After coming up with an idea, developers need to design it. There are a number of different tools you can use for this. The design process is the stuff of other books, but suffice it to say that any functional program must be carefully planned before it can be written.

Step 3: **Code:** The process of writing all of the steps in a detailed design into a *human-readable language* like C, FORTRAN, Pascal, Java, C++, etc. is called coding or programming. This is the process by which programmers write the steps in the algorithm, in a human-readable language. A program in human-readable form is called *source code.*

Step 4: **Translation:** Most humans can't easily read and understand *machine language* or binary (ones 1s and zeros 0s). However, the computer can ONLY understand binary! There are two commonly available types of translation programs available to take human-readable language as input, and produce a machine-readable version of the program: compilers and interpreters. The difference between the two is of no great import right now. The important thing is that all human-readable programs must be translated into executable binary before the computer can use them.

Step 5: **Testing and debugging**: Once the program is coded and translated into binary, it is ready to test. This is a rigorous process that involves running the program with different data samples, and ensuring that the program behaves as expected. If the testing reveals bugs (problems) with the program, development goes back to step 3 and the programmer(s) fix the problem(s). When the bugs have been fixed, the program is retested. When all of the bugs have been fixed, the program is sent on to step 4. Note: Programs will almost always have bugs...totally bug free code is almost impossible to achieve. Some bugs don't appear for years after implementation.

Step 6: **Distribution**: When the program has passed the testing stage, it is ready for public release. At this point there are really only two primary choices: sell it or give it away.

When you buy most software programs, all you are getting is a copy of the binary/executable version. You don't get the source code, because if you had that, you could make some changes, translate your version into binary, and sell your own version! That wouldn't be a good thing for companies like Microsoft because you would be in competition with them! (Interesting tidbit: When you "buy" a program, you don't own the binary you "bought." All you "buy" is the right to use that software on your computer. You can't change, share, sell, or even give away that program. All you can do is use it!) In the case of most Microsoft software, since the license to use the software is usually tied to the serial number of the CPU upon which it is installed, you can't even upgrade your CPU without buying a new license or having an account with Microsoft. This model of computer software is called the *proprietary software* model. The word proprietary means "owned." In this case, the software is actually owned by someone, and you are not that someone!

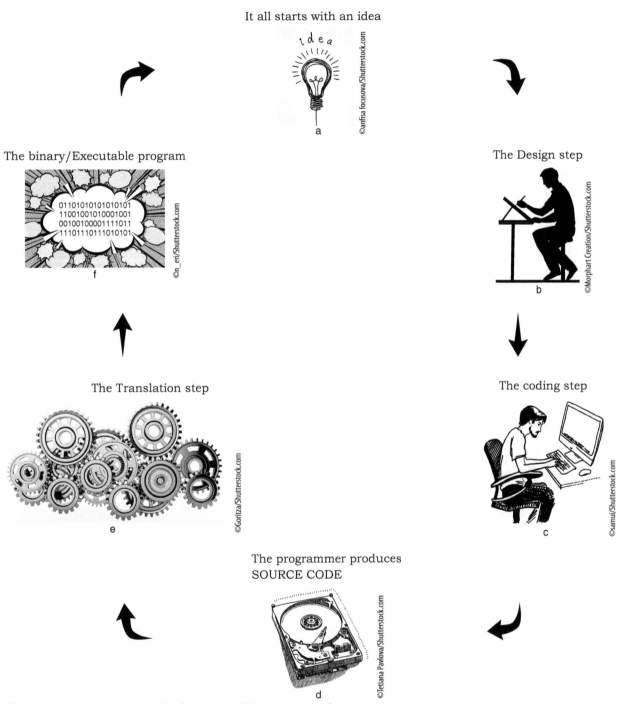

Figure 1   shows an example of the way this process works.

On the other hand, the open source model is very different. As you saw above, when a programmer writes a program, the code/program she creates is crafted in a human-readable language. This is called the *source code*. Open source software allows you to have your very own, personal copy of that source code for the program. That means, if you want to, you can modify the source code, add features, make changes you think would improve the program and create your very own personal, version of the program. On the other hand, you can just run the program as-is. You own a copy of the program. You are free to share it, change it, pass it around, and give it to other people. The only restriction in most cases is that you can't sell it. Freely available source code is very beneficial to you, the user because:

1. There are thousands of people looking at the code. That means there are thousands of people who are looking for, finding, and fixing any problems. There are thousands of people who add improvements and features. And that happens amazingly quickly.

2. Since the source code is available, you don't pay for the programs. They are free. All you have to do is download them and they are yours. However, if you can, there is a moral obligation to give back. If you use open source programs, and you should, and you have the knowledge and skill to improve the programs, you really ought to do so. If you make changes to enhance the program, you should share those improvements with the developers.

I'll give you a real world example of why a rapid reaction to problems is so very important. Back when Microsoft Office 2007 came out, Microsoft changed the *default* file formats from .doc, .xls, and .ppt to .docX, .xlsX, and .pptX. The news at the time reported that they did this because people weren't buying new versions of Office, since the older versions were perfectly adequate for their needs. Because they changed the files default formats, if you had a version of Microsoft Office that was older than the 2007 version, you couldn't even open the newly formatted files! You had to buy the new version of Microsoft Office just to be able to open, edit, and save files in the new format. This drove sales of Office 2007 up. However, that change presented a huge problem for a great number of people, including my faculty peers. The college hadn't upgraded our versions of Office yet, and students who bought new computers or upgraded their version of Office were sending in files that the other instructors couldn't open! Those instructors were forced to email their students and ask them to resend their assignments after saving them in the older formats. You will notice that I said this was a problem for my peers. On the other hand, I had been using LibreOffice for years. Three days after Microsoft announced the new file formats for Office 2007, I received an upgrade for LibreOffice that allowed me to open, read, edit, and save files in the new formats. That's right, just three days after the change was made, I could process the files my students submitted. That kind of rapid response is only possible if there are many, many programmers working on the software.

LibreOffice is an excellent choice for both individuals and companies. It is more robust than Microsoft Office, it is freely available on the Net, and it will be updated much more quickly than proprietary software because so many people have access to the source code. The only real drawbacks to using LibreOffice are the same ones you face with any software package. You need to have a fast enough CPU to run the program. You have to have enough physical storage on your system to store all of the documents you want to keep. And finally, you will only be able to edit the documents that are stored on a physical device connected to your computer. But let's look at a way around even these trivial problems.

GOOGLE DOCS

Suppose you have a little, or an older computer, let's say one with a slow CPU, limited memory, and a small hard drive. And you want to edit a document, say this section of a book. You don't want to buy a new computer...what do you do? You go into the *cloud* and use a package like Google Docs to write and edit your document. Cloud computing, or Software as a Service (SaaS) is the next big evolution of software. When you use Google Docs, the editing program is running on a Google server somewhere in the world, and the document you are creating is being stored on a Google storage server somewhere in the world. You don't know where either of those servers are located. More importantly, you don't even care where they are! All that matters is when you want to edit/read/print the document, it's there and so is the software to perform the required task. More and more companies have started using cloud computing to cut costs and to give their employees access to data wherever they happen to be. In addition to cost savings, another very powerful benefit of cloud editing is that many people can see the document at the same time. For example, when I wrote this section I didn't have to email it to Max, my editor. All I had to do was make it available to him in Google Docs, and he read and edit it to his heart's content (and did a fine job, I might add.) I saw the results of his edits immediately. I didn't have to wait for him to email the edited document back to me. This ability to collaborate on documents, spreadsheets, presentations, etc. is at the heart of cloud-based computing.

Saddleback Leather company is a great example of how cloud computing is an exceptional tool for a progressive and growing company. All of the Saddleback customer service folks have access to a collection of Google Docs. One of them is the file "Customer Requests." When a customer requests that Saddleback start making a new product, let's say dog collars, the customer service representative searches through the "Customer Request" document to see if anyone has requested dog collars before. If someone has, the representative will add one to the number in the column in the document entitled "Request Count," If nobody has asked Saddleback to make dog collars yet, the representative will add "dog collars" to the list of requested products. Since the Customer Requests document is stored in the cloud, all the representatives can see the most current version of the file (since it's the same file!), and keep track of the changes pretty much as they happen. Collaboration is quickly becoming a standard across many industries, and Google Docs is an easy way for companies to provide collaborative tools to their employees.

In addition to creating and editing documents with Google Docs, there is a spreadsheet tool called "Google Sheets," a presentation development program called "Google Slides," and even a tool for making online survey forms called "Google Forms."

In addition to providing tools to process data, Google has "Google Drive" which allows you to store up to 15 gigabytes of data for free! The documents/spreadsheets/presentations you create with the Google tools are also stored on your Google Drive. That way you can access them from any computer that can connect to the Internet. And that is the only significant drawback to using the Google tools—you must have an Internet connection.

Other Choices

Besides LibreOffice, there are a multitude of other programs available to meet your every computational need. (Note: OpenOffice is very similar to LibreOffice, but the two different "branches" feel subtly different. The OpenOffice variants are usually at least one update behind LibreOoffice and it seems that little has been updated since 2014.) There are links to each of them at the end of this section.

BEYOND PRODUCTIVITY SOFTWARE

I don't want to leave you with the idea that the only open source program choices you have involve productivity software. The truth is, there are thousands of open source programs out there for your enjoyment. I will list a few important examples, and provide links at the end of this section so you can go explore others. Some of the programs listed below are not open source, but all are free for download.

Browsers

Another critical class of programs that you will use most every day are browsers. Some of you might think that Internet Explorer (IE) is the only browser available to you. Actually, **IE is the worst choice you can make if you have a PC!** Talk to any cyber-security person and the first thing they will tell you is to NEVER use IE!!! That's because IE is pretty much a magnet for malware. So what other choices do you have? I recommend two, to start with.

Google Chrome

The Google Chrome browser is an amazing tool. It is just one small part of the whole Google ecosystem. I encourage you to go get Chrome, and you might also like tools like Google Earth, Google Maps, Google News, and Google Calendar. If you have a mobile device, Google Maps is an amazing way to navigate when you drive. It not only will give you the best route to your destination, but it also keeps track of traffic, and will route you around delays and traffic jams. I have already mentioned Google Drive and Google Docs. Google Chrome is my day-to-day browser because it has so many features, and because I use so many other Google tools. Granted, Google Chrome isn't open source. It's based on the open-source Chromium project, but is proprietary.

Firefox

This browser is the most recent version of a browser that has been around for a long time. Back in 1998 the Mozilla project was started with the Netscape browser. There have been ups and downs in the process, but the Firefox browser is one of the very best browsers available. In the section on Internet Privacy, you will read that there is a special version of the Firefox browser that uses the Tor network. It's often referred to as the Tor Browser.

Safari

This is the standard Apple browser. It is both robust and secure. If you have an Apple computer, this browser will work well for about 95 percent of the Websites you may wish to visit. I would recommend that even if you have and like Safari, that you download and install one or both of the browsers mentioned above. Like Google Chrome, Safari is free but proprietary.

Other Browsers

There are a veritable plethora of other Web browsers available for your fun and profit. In fact, looking at the major clearing house, Sourceforge, (the address is in the notes at the end of this section), and a search for "Web browsers," returns 2,519 hits! TWO THOUSAND FIVE HUNDRED open source programs that match "Web" and/or "browser"! Good grief! That should give you an idea just how amazing and all-encompassing the open source movement really is!

Additional programs

SourceForge is an absolutely wonderful site to find all kinds of open source software. Here you will find pretty much any kind of software you might want. All of it open source and entirely free. However, one word of warning, not all the programs you find at SourceForge were created equally. Generally the software is safe from malware, but it may not work exactly as you expect it to. You will need to evaluate each of the programs you download to make sure they do what you expect them to. I've never downloaded a "bad" program from Sourceforge but I have had a time or two when I was disappointed with the way a program I downloaded worked... or didn't exactly work.

As more and more programmers continue to contribute code to sites like Source-Forge, the "market" for this type of program continues to grow and expand. Some folks think that "all software should be free," and others believe that any effort by a programmer should result in compensation. Most of us fall somewhere between these two views.

Author's Note: This section, and indeed much of the book, was written using Google Docs. :)

RESOURCES

This page contains links to address the options discussed in this section. They were current as of the publication date of the text. If any of them have suffered from link rot, please just Google the topic to find the most current URLs. Remember, YMMV (Your Mileage May Vary) :)

SourceForge is the premier Website that collects and distributes open source software. There are thousands and thousands of amazing programs available from this site. Pretty much anything you want to do on a computer, any application, will have one (and often many more) programs available for download. One caveat, however; not all these programs are created equally. You may need to download and try several different titles before you find one that works, or works the way you want it to. In the parlance of white hat hackers, YMMV. Before you spend your hard earned dollars on proprietary software, I humbly suggest you take a look at what's available at SourceForge. You just may find exactly what you are looking for, and save a few Bitcoin in the bargain. https://sourceforge.net/

LibreOffice is the most highly recommended of the free software suites. If you are trying to stay away from Microsoft products, most sources agree that LibreOffice is your best choice. http://www.libreoffice.org

Google Docs (and the assorted other Google apps) are ideal for almost all common productivity needs. There are a large number of Google apps available. I recommend you check all of them out. https://www.google.com/docs/about/

Zoho is a comprehensive business solution—it is much more than a regular office suite. You may find it useful: https://home.zoho.com/home

Jarte is a free suite, and you can buy additional bells and whistles if you wish. http://www.jarte.com/

Google Chrome is my recommended Web browser for the majority of sites. It is one of the two standard browsers I think all computer users should have available. In addition to being a top notch browser, using Chrome opens up a whole universe of Google programs, many of which you will find invaluable once you begin to use them.

Firefox is the other standard browser I encourage you to download and use. It is the end product of a long and proud development effort that started with Netscape back in the early 90s. Firefox is my other "go to" browser besides Chrome. The interfaces are slightly different, and Firefox has a wealth of add-ons to enhance your browsing experience. There is even a variant of Firefox that uses the Tor network instead of the surface web. I explain the whole idea of Tor in another section. For now, all you need to know is that by using the Tor variant of the Firefox browser, your browsing behavior will be pretty close to anonymous.

GLOSSARY

Word / Phrase	Definition
Cloud	The cloud is a fancy way to say Internet. The idea either comes from physics and the way electrons are distributed about the nucleus of an atom in an electron cloud or it came from the clouds that network engineers used to depict areas for which the structure was unknown or irrelevant, like the Internet. But, I digress, you don't have to know physics to use cloud-based services like Google Docs. With cloud-based computing you have no idea where the machine that is processing your document is in the real world. Nor do you have any idea where you document is being stored. Nor should you care! All that matters is when you want to read/edit/open the document the software and the document are available.
Default File Formats	A default is the option you get if you don't make a choice. While you have a couple of dozen possible file formats in Microsoft Word, if you don't pick one of those formats you get what is called the default file format. For example, in the South, if you order ice tea you get sweet tea. But up North, if you order ice tea, you get unsweetened tea. So, in the South, sweet tea is the "default."
Human-Readable Language	This term refers to one of the myriad of programming languages used to write computer programs. This is also called the "source code." Before the computer can run a program, it must be translated into machine language, or binary. There are a plethora of human readable languages used to craft computer programs. Contrast this with "Machine language." See "Source code."
Machine Language	This refers to binary. Ones and zeros. This is the only language a computer can understand. Programs must be translated from human-readable language to machine language before they can be executed or run. Other terms for this version of a program are: binary, executable, runnable.
Open Source	Programs and/or documents that are made available, usually on the Net, that allow you to see, modify and save the human-readable version of the program. Most often, this refers to programs that provide either the executable version (binary) alongside human-readable (source) versions or just the human-readable (source). These programs are typically distributed free of charge. You will need to have the proper software to edit the code provided.

Proprietary Software	Software that is sold for profit. This describes most of the commercial software available today. Part of the End User License Agreement you routinely "accept" without reading contains a clause that forbids your trying to reverse engineer the binary to recreate the source code. It is important that you realize that when you "buy" a proprietary software package all you actually own is the right to use that software. You do not own the actual binary!
Software Suite	This term describes a collection of software that is bundled together and designed to work together. One advantage of acquiring a software suite is that the interface for all the programs in the suite will be similar. Usually all the programs will work together by sharing data and other content as well.
Source Code	Another name for the human-readable version of a program. The source code is the source that describes exactly what the program will do. Source code is often editable. Most source code can be edited, or changed, to give the program more features, to fix bugs or errors in programming, or to simply make the program run more efficiently.

Electronic Books (The Good, the Bad, and the Ugly)

So what is all the fuss about these new-fangled electronic books? Why are they amazingly popular with some readers? What are the advantages of not having to lug around old, dusty, heavy paper-and-cardboard tomes? Why have Barnes and Nobles and Amazon sold millions and millions of Nooks Kindles? Why are the projected ebook sales worldwide for 2016 estimated to exceed 15 million dollars? Why do ebook sales account for over twenty percent of all book sales in the United States? And then, what about the other side of the whole ebook concept? What are the disadvantages to using ebooks? Are there learning problems associated with ebooks? Why would I or you not want an etextbook?

Wow, those are really good questions! Let's look at why ebooks seem to be so popular and then let's also look at the dark side of ebooks. That way we can have a fair and balanced discussion about the whole topic, and you can decide for yourself whether ebooks are for you. You will be able to determine when using an ebook is appropriate and when it might not be the best choice to make.

So we are all on the same page, for purposes of this discussion I'll define an ebook as any electronically stored or delivered content in either visual or auditory format.

That means that audio books fall under this general category as well as books formatted to be read on a Kindle, Nook, tablet, phone, or any other computer.

THE PLUS SIDE OF EBOOKS

There are a number of really good reasons why ebooks are so popular, both with readers and authors. Let's take a look at some of the more obvious of these.

1. Ebooks are easy to carry. A book in electronic format, not including the weight of the reader, actually weights very, very little. Physically, a book stored as an ebook is just some electrons tucked away in your reader's storage. Electrons don't weigh all that much. Technically, an electron weighs about 9.109×10^{-31} kilograms. So even hundreds of thousands of them won't weigh you down very much. Actually, you probably won't be able to tell the difference between the weight of your ebook reader when it is brand new and empty, and that same reader when it has hundreds of books stored on it. According to the research, the increase in the weight of a Kindle empty, and a fully loaded Kindle is around 10^{-18} grams. That sure beats having to haul around half-a-dozen or more textbooks that each weigh several pounds! The charge in the ereader battery actually weighs more than all of the possible ebooks that could be stored on the device!

2. Electronic books take up very little space. Now, I must confess that I am a dyed-in-the-wool bibliophile. I, personally, love books! I like writing books, I like reading books, I like the feel of a well-bound book in my hands. I even love the smell of a new, leather-bound book. The problem comes when I have to find a place to put all my lovely books. Since I have over 3000 hardcover books, a significant part of my home is taken up by my library. Many, many bookshelves all full of beautiful books. Books that have to be dusted. Books that need to be rearranged when I acquire new titles. Books that will have to be moved if I ever move. (Oh good Lord, spare me having to move them!) That is a huge mass of paper, and each tome is special to me. I could put most if not all of the same content on an ebook reader, or in the worst case maybe a reader and an external hard disk drive or even a 256-GB SD card. That would save me a lot of space, a lot of hauling, a lot of dusting! On the other hand, unless I use a digital certificate, it's really hard to have an author sign an electronic copy of a first edition of her book!

3. Along the same lines, electronic books are more "green" than traditional ink and paper books. Nobody has to cut down a tree to make an electronic book. No critters need to be skinned to bind an ebook. Ebooks don't end up taking up room in a land fill. (Well, if the thumb drive the ebooks are on gets thrown away, I guess then they would take up a wee bit of space in a land fill, but the effect of that on the environment would be miniscule.) Electronic books

are much more ecologically sound than any of my dusty old tomes. Ebooks are good for the environment, at least until you need to recycle your ebook reader. There is one more ecological consideration, however. Electronic book readers do require electricity while none is required to read a paper book, at least during daylight. It is possible to kill trees if you want a hard copy or printed copy of your ebook. But at least in the US, this is generally considered copyright infringement, and I've never seen an ereader make it easy... usually involves taking screenshots and emailing them to yourself or some similar sort of hassle.

4. The cost of ebooks is another significant factor in their popularity. For example, the excellent and frightening fiction book "Drone Command" by Mike Maden costs $27.00 in hardcover format on Amazon.com. The Kindle edition of the same book only costs $13.99. The ebook costs about half what the hardcover version costs and contains exactly the same words. In addition, I will have to pay shipping and handling to get the hardcover edition of the book, but downloading the ebook doesn't cost anything. So if I want to collect hardcover editions of all of Mike's books, I'll have to spend a fair amount of my hard-earned money. I could get the same content for just a shade over half as much, and I would get every one of the same words to enjoy. This print upcharge can be even more of a consideration when buying textbooks. On the other hand, this isn't always the case as we will see when we look at the dark side of ebooks.

5. Another great advantage of electronic books is how quickly I can get them. Suppose that this evening I finish Mike's book "Blue Warrior," and I want to read "Drone Command," the third book in the series. If I am using my ebook reader, I can pay for "Drone Command," and have it downloaded before I finish making a nice cup of tea to enjoy as I read. On the other hand, if I limit myself to hardcover books, then I have to wait at least two days, even if I have Amazon Prime, before I can continue the story. Two whole days! Good grief! Two days of staring at the wall wishing my new book would get here. Yes, getting the next book in the series in a matter of minutes can make a huge difference in my composure. LOL

6. The table of contents in some electronic books is "clickable." That means I can instantly go to any section or even any specific page in an ebook much more quickly than I could in a paper book. Also, if the ebook is well designed, key words might be configured to be links to their definitions. Additionally, the Amazon Kindle app makes it possible to look up any word in Merriam-Webster by tapping and holding on the word. That means I wouldn't have to flip back to the glossary (or worse, grab a dictionary!) to find out what some technical word means.

7. As the technology improves, reading an ebook becomes more and more comparable with reading from paper. The early ebooks were far too bright, and the pixel density wasn't all that great so the characters were difficult to make out. A lot of people got headaches after reading from them for even a sort time. That has changed to some extent. Now the hardware and the associated software have improved so much that some folks think that reading from a screen is almost as comfortable as good old paper (there is research that both confirms and contradicts this). In addition, the ability of some e-readers to zoom in, making the text larger on the screen, is a boon to older readers and those with vision challenges.

8. There are a lot of free ebooks available on the Internet. A LOT of free books! It has become a way for aspiring writers, and writers who can't find a publisher to build a following. As a side-note, services like CreateSpace also allow writers without publishers to publish their books in print format and distribute through Amazon with limited financial investment. Some groups have put a fair number of older books, books that have gone out of print and books with expired copyrights, out on the Net for free. If you do a Google search for "Free eBooks" you will find about 103,000,000 results. Some of them list how many books are available. For example, just one site, "www.gutenberg.org" claims to have 45,000 free books available! 45,000 books! Wow, reading all of those would take you a couple of weekends at least!

9. Ebooks, in audio form, allow the "reader" to do other things while "reading" the book. "Books on tape" provide excellent books that you can listen to while working out, walking, or doing other menial tasks that don't require your full attention.

10. As was mentioned in the previous point, anyone with access to a computer and the Net can become an e-author. Amazon.com is one of the prominent online retailers. They support the Kindle devices and applications, so they want your book in a format that is Kindle-friendly. They also have a whole service set up to help authors self-publish their work. Kindle Direct Publishing (KDP) provides all of the tools an aspiring author needs to become published. There are really just three major steps involved in using KDP to bring your amazing words to your eager audience.

   A. Prepare your manuscript in a word processor. KDP provides tools to incorporate many different file types, but it is easiest to use a program like LibreOffice to create a .doc or .docx version of your manuscript. Once you have your manuscript ready to go, Amazon claims it takes less than five minutes to get your document uploaded and converted (assuming no formatting issues) and it will be available to your audience in 24 to 72 hours.

B. Publish your book on KDP. Once you upload your manuscript, the KDP software will automatically reformat it for the Kindle reader. Then all you have to do is create the cover, verify that you have permissions to use the material uploaded, and set the price for your book. According to Amazon, self-publishing on Amazon allows you to receive as much as 70% royalties on your book. (But beware, this 70% number is misleading marketing—using the maximum profit amount, Amazon pays 70% minus significant fees for product delivery, especially for large books or those with images, which chew through artificially-priced data.) As they say, YMMV (Your Mileage May Vary). Traditional publishing usually only provides 10–15% royalties, so self-publishing might give you greater return per book sold.

C. Promote your book. Let people know what it is about and where they can find it. You might consider using social media to let the world know of your magnificent manifesto, or you could, I suppose, spam all your contacts with the purchase information. I wouldn't recommend the latter, but it has been done in the past. There is a link in the references section that goes over these steps in great detail in case you are ready to release your opus to the world.

11. Electronic books can have additional content embedded within the text. For example, an ebook about origami could have videos embedded within it that would show you how to make specific folds. That's pretty hard to do with a paper and ink book!

A final advantage of the electronic book is that, should your taste in literature (and I use the term very loosely) run to the less than socially acceptable, well, nobody can tell exactly what you are reading on your ereader. There is no lurid cover to give you away. You can even read books with such lascivious content as cryptography, tensor calculus, or even this text with complete assurance that those in your immediate vicinity will have no clue as to your sordid predilections.

THE DARK SIDE OF EBOOKS....

Right off the bat, I realize that this part of this section might seem strange to those, hopefully few, of you who are reading this on an ebook reader. As of this writing, my publisher will allow this treatise to only be available in hard-copy. To be fair, I must also admit that as a bibliophile I find ebooks to be an anathema. I like good old paper books. Books you can cuddle up with on a cold winter's night in front of the fireplace. Although I do have and love an iPad Air, I don't have any books on it, and I really can't bring myself to cuddle up to it. OK, having confessed those biases, let's look at the problems that have been discovered with reading from electronic books, especially textbooks in electronic format. Some of these problems might not be too important if all you use your ebook for is pleasure reading...but, hey, do you really read textbooks for pleasure and fun?

So what are the problems associated with reading technical/serious material presented in electronic format? There are a number of problems that are less than obvious, and some that pretty much make ebooks impractical for serious reading... if you want to remember what you read. First, let's look at the elephant in the room.

1. Ereaders might be OK for reading fiction, but they are not a good choice if you want to learn and remember what you read. Because ebooks are on a screen, reading them engages a different part of your brain than reading the same material from a paper document. I realize that sounds odd, but when you read from a screen you actually use a different part of your brain to process the data. There are numerous studies that show that when you read from a screen you engage in what is called "non-linear reading" the way you typically read a Web page. Your eyes skim over the words, and move about the screen in a seemingly haphazard fashion.

   "Deep reading" is just the opposite. When you deep read, you immerse yourself in the text. That's the way you read a novel when you really get into it. That's the way you read a contract or other legal document. And that type of reading requires practice or you will gradually lose the ability! Deep reading enables you to learn and retain information. On the other hand, non-linear reading makes it difficult to follow the thread of an argument, or to let an author help you reach a point of understanding. If you spend most of your reading time using nonlinear techniques, you will find it more and more difficult to engage in deep reading. Unfortunately, studying involves deep reading. Researchers also discovered that when people are reading nonlinearly, they are much more prone to distraction. This is especially true if you are not using a dedicated ebook reader. For example, if you were reading this on your laptop, desktop, iPad, etc. you might well be distracted by a text message popping up, or a Facebook notification, etc. On the other hand, if you are curled up in your favorite chair, with your ink and paper book, in front of the fire, you will most likely keep reading instead of checking your computer. So while ebooks offer a myriad of features like convenience, portability, and price, research shows that it probably isn't a good idea to get your textbooks in electronic format.

2. Taking notes, especially marginal notes, is very difficult if not impossible with most ereaders. Some folks who use a tablet like an iPad to read their electronic texts can open a word processor as well, and use the word processor to keep

notes. However, this has proven to be a difficult practice because it requires the reader to switch from one application to another. They are forced to switch from the reader to the word processor and back, time and time again. Most people find this so clumsy that they just stop taking notes. Yet taking notes has proven to be a very important part of learning material. Most of my technical books are filled with my annotations, my questions, and my notes to myself. Those notes are very valuable when I need to go back to review a particular subject that I haven't consulted recently. Some of the ereaders allow you to highlight lines of text, which might help you find a particular passage, but the lack of marginal note-taking tools is a major drawback for technical (or college) study.

3. It takes 20 to 30 percent more time to read the same material on an ebook instead of from a paper book. That means that it will take you significantly longer to read this same section if you are reading it on an ebook. College students are usually pressed for time, so increasing the amount of time you have to spend reading your textbook is not a good thing! In addition, if you budget a fixed amount of time each day to read, which, by the way, you should, then you will cover 20 to 30 percent less material during that time if you are reading from an ebook. Yikes!

4. Reading from a screen requires measurably more cognitive functioning than reading the same material from paper. It also causes stress, and leads more quickly to mental exhaustion than reading from a physical book. So you have to invest more mental effort to read from your ebook than you would have to if you were reading from an ink-and-paper textbook. In addition, careful research into the mental effects of reading from a screen have shown that people who read from a screen are more often depressed than their peers who read exactly the same content from physical books.

5. Another study demonstrated that the size of the screen has a major effect upon the reader's ability to recall the material she read. The smaller the screen, the worse the recall. So it's a bad idea to try to read your textbook on your smartphone. Your recall will be better on a tablet like an iPad, but even then it will still be significantly lower than if you had read the same material on paper. And good grief, imagine how difficult it would be to recall information read on an Apple watch! In addition, regardless of screen orientation and background brightness, reading from even the best ereader causes eye strain.

6. (Note: I realize that in point 7 of the pro-ebook part of this section I said the some folks feel that ereaders have gotten better. They have, but spending time reading from an electronic text still causes eye-strain, just not as quickly as with the early ereaders.) Some of the research into how much you

can remember from reading an electronic text has to do with additional cues you get from a paper book that can't be duplicated on a screen. These cues, called spatial orientation, include: where the words appear on the page, the tactile effects of turning physical pages, and whether the text is on the right or left page. While these differences seem paltry at first, the research shows that all of these positional cues do effect how much you remember about the subject of your study.

7. Then there are the practical problems associated with using ebooks. Problems like the need for a power source, the requirement of a working WiFi connection (for some platforms' DRM, and for acquiring new content). Both the ambient light and surrounding point source lights can make it very difficult to read the text because of screen glare or washout of the text on the screen. In addition, not all etexts are formatted to run on all of the different device families. For example, books formatted for the Kindle clan, like .azw, usually can't be read on any of the other ereaders. By my count, here in mid-2016, there are over 30 different formats for electronic book content, and only a couple of them, like .txt (plain text) and .pdf (portable document format) are readable across all the current readers. And neither of those formats are very pretty to read. Especially .txt which looks like Figure 1!

```
This is an example of a plain text file,
extension (.txt).  There isn't much
formatting, the font is really limited,
and all in all it is a pretty ugly piece
of work.
```

Figure 1   Text formatted in .txt format. Not all that pretty or fun to read

8. Another downside to buying ebooks is the cost. While there is no paper-and-ink involved, and no trees need be harvested to create an ebook, the price often isn't all that much lower than the print and paper version. This, unfortunately, is especially true for textbooks. For example, the print version of the latest edition of the book "CMPTR", an introduction to computers text-book, costs $99.95 on Amazon.com. On the other hand, the Kindle edition only costs $99.95 to buy and a mere $77.04 to rent. Some people are upset that the cost of an ebook, which doesn't have to be printed, is so close to the cost of the hard copy print and paper edition. What most folks don't realize is that the actual printing costs for a textbook only make up about eight percent of the total production costs. Regardless of the format, books must be edited, they must be composited, and they must be advertised and distributed. All of those things make up a much larger portion of the total

production cost compared to the printing costs. So looking at the CMPTR book, if they sold the ebook at a price that reflected the actual savings, the ebook version would only be about $8.00 cheaper than the print version.

All in all, using an ebook version of a textbook is fraught with problems. You will have to read the text more times, it will take you longer to read the text each time, you won't recall nearly as much material from your reading, and the cost isn't that much better than the good, old, paper-and-ink textbook that you are, hopefully, reading right now!

So while there are some really good features of ebooks, features that make them more convenient, more portable, and at least slightly less expensive; it probably isn't a good idea to get your textbooks in electronic format. On the other hand, it may be cost and bulk effective to buy fiction books in the electronic format. You can store several hundred or even thousands of books on your ereader, and they don't weigh you down at all. I recommend that if you want to buy an ereader, and start reading "books" in that format, that you limit yourself to only books you don't care about remembering. And even then, some readers have trouble remembering characters' names and plot lines in electronic books. Of course the choice is yours, and I hope this section has given you enough hard data to make the best choice for your style of learning.

REFERENCES

Deep Reading: http://www.pri.org/stories/2014-09-18/your-paper-brain-and-your-kindle-brain-arent-same-thing

http://healthland.time.com/2012/03/14/do-e-books-impair-memory/

http://www.theguardian.com/books/2014/aug/19/readers-absorb-less-kindles-paper-study-plot-ereader-digitisation

http://www.aallnet.org/mm/Publications/spectrum/archives/vol-17/No-2/e-book-disadvantages.pdf

http://www.apartmenttherapy.com/e-readers-pros-cons-218010

http://tablets-textbooks.procon.org/#background

Weight of ebooks in a reader: http://www.nytimes.com/2011/10/25/science/25qna.html?_r=0

Self-publishing: https://kdp.amazon.com/help?topicId=A2VHRJZXET0TWT

RFID (Radio Frequency IDentification)

Radio Frequency Identification (RFID) is a very powerful technology that has revolutionized our lives. We use this technology daily. It makes our lives less complex, makes us more productive, and enables forms of technology otherwise impossible. For example, tracking library books, handling border crossings (your passport has an RFID tag now), preventing shoplifting, allowing you to buy gas without going into the station or even opening your wallet;), giving you access to buildings, letting you pay tolls without even slowing down; the list goes on and on. Let's look first at the history of RFID, a history that goes back a LOT further than most of us realize.

While electromagnetic energy has been part of the world, well, since its creation, it wasn't until 1887 that the German physicist Heinrich Hertz determined that electromagnetic energy moves in waves at the speed of light. In 1896, the Italian physicist Guglielmo Marconi was able to send a "wireless" or radio message across the Atlantic Ocean, and the age of rapid information transmission was born. Then, in 1906, Ernst Alexanderson was able to generate continuous radio waves, which allowed both true radio communication as well as the first true use of RFID, RADAR (RAdio Detection And Ranging).

RADAR was first used in 1922. The actual details of the development of RADAR are shrouded in secrecy because it was developed to detect enemy airplanes during the World War II. In general, it works by transmitting high-frequency radio waves, and then detecting when/if they are reflected from an object back to the RADAR antenna. In addition to determining if an object exists, the time it takes for the radio waves to go to the object and back, is used to calculate the speed and direction of the object. This can tell a RADAR operator how far away an object is, and how fast that object is moving. Yup, this is the same kind of RADAR officer friendly uses to see if you are speeding. Aren't you glad this technology was invented? LOL The problem with this technology was that while you could see if something was coming at you, and how fast it was coming, you couldn't tell if it was one of the good guys, or one of the bad guys. This led to the development of the IFF (Identify Friend or Foe) *transponder*. An IFF transponder receives the RADAR (radio) waves from the RADAR transmitter, and returns a radio signal that uniquely identifies the aircraft or other object. If you have seen video of an air traffic control screen, the little numbers and letters next to each of the moving "dots" on the screen are the data sent by the IFF system. Figure 1 shows an example of an air traffic RADAR screen.

©AndreyVP/Shutterstock.com

Figure 1   A sample air traffic control screen

RADAR was the first large scale use of radio waves to identify an object at a distance. Since then, this same technology has been put to use in many, many ways. It is the same technology, after much development, that a veterinarian uses to identify your precious puppy using the data on the "chip" you have had implanted in her. That "chip" is nothing more than a little RFID transponder that receives the signal from the scanner and returns a unique number that can be used to identify your pup and her owner. Using those data the two of you can be reunited should she wander away from her home. As you can see, it is something like the IFF transponder in airplanes, except in this case the RFID chip will only send a number to the scanner. That number is a reference to an entry in a database kept by the company that made the chip. When you registered your pup, the veterinarian sent your contact information to the chip's manufacturer. Those data were entered into the database so if someone calls the company with the number returned by the chip, the company can provide your contact information so you can get your puppy back. As an aside, be sure to update those contact data if you move, change your phone number, etc. It would be really terrible if animal control captured your dog, but the contact data were incorrect so they couldn't get her back to you!

An interesting bit of serendipity: the development of microwave ovens came from observations made by RADAR operators. You see, a microwave oven is nothing more than a radio transmitter that broadcasts radio waves that match the *resonant frequency* of water molecules. When those molecules are bombarded with radio waves of a specific frequency (2.45 GHz) they vibrate more violently. The vibrations create friction among the adjacent molecules which translates into heat, and the heat cooks your food. Percy Spencer, a Raytheon employee, made this serendipitous discovery. He noticed that when he was in front of a small RADAR dish that was transmitting, the candy bar in his pocket melted! That observation, and the intelligence to recognize it for what it was, resulted in a completely new way to prepare food! The first commercial microwave ovens were even called "RADAR ranges."

First, let's look at the way the most common sort of RFID chip works. This type of chip is called a *passive RFID chip* because it only sends out its data when it is queried or asked for them. Another type of chip, called an *active RFID chip,* that we will look at shortly.

Look at Figure 2.

The dark square in the middle is the actual RFID chip. The lines that surround it are a copper foil antenna. When the chip is bombarded with radio waves of the correct frequency, like those generated by a scanner, the radio waves create a small electric current in the antenna. That current powers up the chip and it broadcasts the data stored on it. In the case of your puppy, the data are just a number that uniquely identifies that chip and identifies a file in the company's database where your contact data are kept. Other types of RFID chip can store and transmit up to 2,000 bytes of data.

One of the first commercial uses for RFID technology was theft deterrence. In the 1960s, scientists developed what was called a "1-bit tag." As its name implies,

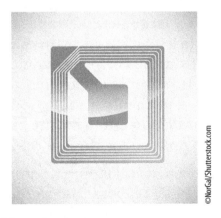

©NorGal/Shutterstock.com

Figure 2   A simple, passive RFID chip and antenna

this tag was set either on or off (1 or 0). When attached to merchandise, the tag was activated, or set to 1. When the customer purchased that item the tag was turned off (set to 0) at the checkout stand. As the customer left the store, he went through a tag reader at the door. The reader would send a signal to the tag, and the tag would respond with its value. If the tag had been turned off, nothing would happen, but if the tag was still set to one, an alarm would sound.

RFID development in the 1970s primarily focused on ways of tracking things. Companies in the US needed to keep track of things like railroad cars. In Europe, the focus was on tracking livestock. There were also some early efforts to create tags that would let users use toll roads, bridges, and tunnels without having to stop and pay tolls.

In the 1980s, the United States research focused primarily on transportation and personal access, while in Europe the focus was still on animals, especially tracking cattle. The late 1980s saw the first successful, commercial use of this technology to manage toll roads, parking garages, and some limited on-street parking. One of the early implementations was the Toll Tag in the Dallas/Ft. Worth metroplex. A single tag, with its embedded RFID chip, allowed drivers to drive on certain toll roads, and access parking at the Dallas/Ft. Worth and Love Field airports without ever using any cash or even opening their wallets. These tags also allowed access to several parking garages in the downtown Dallas area, and even access to some specific gated communities.

By the 1990s, RFID was in such widespread use that it became necessary to create a set of standards allowing chips from different manufactures to communicate. One of the major focuses for research at this time was toll collection. Toll companies only make money when cars pass through toll booths. If there were a way to collect tolls without making the driver stop and wait on a person to take their money, more cars could use the road, generating more income for the toll company. In the days before RFID based toll tags, one of the first attempts trying to keep traffic moving involved large net-like bins at toll booths. Drivers would slow down some, and toss their change into the bin. An automatic coin sorter checked that the driver had paid the correct amount. If the amount was correct, the machine lifted a barrier. However, this still required the driver to slow down enough to throw his change, and then wait for the barrier to lift. In addition, it required the driver to be accurate enough to hit the bin with the change! Alas, this didn't speed up toll collection enough for the toll road companies.

The major breakthrough happened in Oklahoma in 1991. One of the Oklahoma toll road companies installed RFID readers that were powerful and fast enough to capture the data from RFID chips placed on the cars themselves. This permitted the driver to blow through the toll booth at highway speeds without ever slowing down at all. Of course there were video cameras set up to capture images of the license plate and face of the drivers for cars that weren't yet equipped with the RFID chips. Since the cars never stopped or even slowed down, many more vehicles could use the toll road without congestion. More vehicles moving through the toll booths (readers) more quickly meant more income for the company that owned the toll road.

In 1992 the Harris County Toll Road Authority began using RFID chips to both collect tolls and implement traffic management systems. Now the term "traffic management" sounds pretty benign, doesn't it? Unfortunately, what it describes is using toll tags to monitor each car's speed, and issue tickets by mail to drivers who were speeding! For example, if car A passed the first tag reader at 9:21 AM, and passed the second tag reader at 9:23 AM, and the two readers were 3 miles apart, how fast was the car going? Yes, this is one of those challenging "story problems" from math class! Anyway, 3 miles in 2 minutes means 1.5 miles per minute (3 divided by 2). Multiply 1.5 miles/hour by 60 (minutes in an hour), and you get 90 miles per hour. Yikes! So, a technology designed to save you time on the toll road became a technology that invaded your privacy and possibly resulted in your getting a ticket. For those of us who, from time to time, consider the speed limit signs as suggestions rather than absolutes, this is a **bad thing**! This is yet another example of a neutral technology used for "evil"...at least in my humble opinion.

Another major breakthrough happened in 1999. The Uniform Code Council, Proctor & Gamble, Gillette, and EAN (European Article Number organization) established the Auto-ID Center at the Massachusetts Institute of Technology. The mission of the center was two-fold; first they needed to develop a set of standards so diverse companies could employ RFID tags and readers made by multiple vendors. Next they were to develop low-cost RFID tags that could be used to identify individual retail products. Those tags provided a way to track individual items through the whole supply chain from creation to sale (and unfortunately beyond). This was a significant change in the way RFID was used, and in the way the world looked at the uses of RFID. Prior to this, the RFID tag contained a lot of data, and they were fairly large; about the size of a playing card. The Auto-ID Center developed the first generation of the tiny, inexpensive tags that could be used to identify pretty much every product imaginable. This was the beginning of the invasion of RFID technology into our everyday lives.

By 2003, most of the major retailers and big-box stores like Walmart, Metro, Target, and Albertsons had embraced the technology. Even the U.S. Department of Defense had begun to use RFID to track materiel through the different logistical channels from supplier all the way to the individual soldier who ended up using it. By 2005, Walmart required all of its top 100 suppliers to tag each of their products before delivering them to the Walmart warehouses. A couple of years ago I spoke with the manager of my local Walmart, and she explained that every single product valued over $50 had an RFID tag installed somewhere on or in it. The expansion of RFID implementation on products that are integrated into our daily lives has literally exploded. Let's look at some of the pros and cons of this amazing, powerful, invasive, and frightening technology.

POSITIVE USES OF RFID

I will give you an overview of some of the more common uses for RFID technology that you will most likely encounter in your daily life. There are, of course many implementations of RFID that you never even notice. This list represents just the tip of the RFID iceberg. I am also not going to try to envision the potential and probable deployments of RFID in the future. I don't want to scare you too badly!

You get up in the morning and greet the day with a cup of coffee and a bowl of cereal. It is likely that the container of coffee beans has an embedded RFID tag somewhere in or on the container. Likewise, there is a good chance your cereal box is also tagged. Inventory control and tracking is one of the very best uses of RFID technology. So let's track that bag of coffee beans from the roaster to your cup. When the roaster bags their freshly roasted coffee beans, the bags most likely have an embedded RFID chip. After filling a pallet with bags, the roaster wraps the whole pallet in plastic and prepares to send it to the wholesaler. Instead of counting the individual bags of beans, the roaster simply rolls the pallet past an RFID scanner. In milliseconds, the scanner automatically identifies each tag and records the number and type of bags on the pallet. Besides a count, the scanner also pulls the roasting date from the chip. When the trucking company comes by to pick up the pallet of beans, their driver uses a mobile scanner to "count" the number of bags on the pallet as well. He compares his count with the roaster's count to make sure all the bags are accounted for. When the pallet of beans arrives at the warehouse, it is again rolled past a scanner that identifies the number, type, age, size, and flavor of each bag of beans and posts those data to the warehouse's server. Your local retailer has ordered ten bags of a particular flavor of beans from the warehouse, so one of the warehouse employees opens the plastic wrap on the pallet and removes the ten bags. Those bags are again scanned to make sure they are of the correct type and that the count is correct. When the beans arrive at your retailer, they are again scanned into the shop's inventory and the data are stored on the shop's database. Since coffee beans have shelf life of six to nine months, each time the store takes inventory the managers can determine whether it is time to remove older bags from the shelf based on the roasting date stored on the chip. When you buy a bag of your favorite beans, the RFID tag on the bag is scanned at checkout, and the store's inventory count for that particular flavor of bean is automatically reduced by the number of bags you bought. If you have your own RFID reader, you can then scan the chip on the bag to make sure the beans are fresh and of the correct flavor. (Note: most of us don't have a home scanner, yet, but that technology is coming!)

Wow, that little RFID chip sure gets a lot of exercise! The coffee bean example shows you the path that most goods take. It illustrates how RFID technology is used. Inventory tracking and control is an outstanding use for RFID technology. That was one of the first uses for the technology, and is very important in today's supply chain management. When the RFID roll-out is completed, almost every item on every shelf in almost all the stores you shop in will be wearing its own RFID tag! Even the individual bottles of Dr. Pepper in a six-pack will have an identification tag, probably molded into the cap.

OK, it's time to leave for work or school. As you drive out of your neighborhood, you notice that you are low on gas, so you stop by your local Exxon gas station. When you pull up to the pump, and get out of your car, the pump scans the RFID chip in the Speedpass on your keychain. Since the Speedpass is linked to your credit card, the pump knows what account to bill for your gas purchase.

Driving along, you notice that the freeway you normally take is a bit backed up, and since you are almost running late, you don't have time to sit in a traffic jam. Instead of taking your usual route, you jump on the tollway. As you cruise along, RFID readers scan your toll tag and bill the credit card associated with your account. You don't have to slow down, you don't have to dig out your wallet and pay a toll, you just zip along and the tolls are collected automatically.

When you arrive at your destination, the parking gate automatically opens for you when the RFID reader reads the chip in your parking pass. You don't even have to plug your ID card into the reader, it's done at a distance. Heck, you don't even need to slow down. Although it might be a good idea to. When you approach your building, the door lock reads the RFID chip in your employee/student badge and automatically unlocks the door for you. It also records when and by which door you entered the building so you don't have to punch a time clock. Depending upon the sophistication of your company's RFID system, it may even keep track of exactly where you are in the building by keeping track of your ID badge. In some companies, the system is good enough to route phone calls to the phone nearest you if you get an incoming call. When you go to lunch in the cafeteria you don't pay for your lunch with cash, the register has an RFID reader that automatically scans the chip in your credit card. At the end of the day, it's the reverse of your morning trip. The freeway is even more crowded, so you again take the toll road. Stopping at your local grocery store you pick up a couple of items for dinner and again your credit card is scanned from a distance to you don't even have to take the card out of your wallet.

Arriving home you discover that your cat must have snuck outside as you left in the morning. She was, unfortunately, apprehended by your local animal control officer. Since you had the foresight to have her "chipped," there is a message on your phone asking you to come pick her up at the local shelter. After retrieving your wayward pet, you spend a quiet night at home.

As you can see from the description above, our daily lives are made easier and more efficient because so many things we use every day include an RFID chip. There are a myriad of other applications for RFID technology as well. Let's look at some excellent uses for this technology.

TRACKING CRITTERS

It's not only dogs and cats that can wear an RFID identity chip. (By the way, I urge you to please have your pets chipped. It's only right that should they become lost you can give them the very best chance to be reunited with you!) The technology is critical to keeping track of other animals as well. Many cattle ranchers chip each of their cows/bulls/steers so they can keep track of any health problems, vaccination records, etc. RFID chips allow ranchers to identify valuable stolen or lost cattle if the chip is actually implanted into the animal. The early tags were too large to implant, and were attached to the cow's ear. Newer tags are so small (about the size of a grain of rice) that it is more efficient and practical to embed the chips under the animal's skin. Researchers have also tagged wild animals with RFID chips to track their migratory movements or to establish their natural range. These tags are known as *active RFID tags* because they contain a transmitter and a power source so that they can regularly send out a signal instead of waiting to be activated by a radio broadcast. The miniaturization of this technology has reached the point that researchers can place an active RFID chip on individual honey bees!

This technology is also used to track people! Some companies ask that their employees have passive RFID chips implanted in their hands, instead of issuing them a badge with a chip. They use the embedded chip just like the chip on a card to grant access, track the employee through the facility, etc. Security is the primary advantage of embedding the chip instead of issuing a badge. An implanted chip is difficult to lose, leave at home, or have stolen. In cultures where it is common practice to kidnap people, especially children, an embedded, active RFID chip can help the police track and recover the child. One of the especially beneficial uses for this technology is tracking elderly people with Alzheimer's or other mental problems that cause them to wander. If your wandering elder has an active RFID chip implanted, you can set up a virtual perimeter around their house. If your elder strays outside that perimeter, monitoring software can send you an email, text, or even call you and show you the current location of your elder on a map. This technology has proven to be a life saver in dozens of cases.

TRACKING INVENTORY

We already saw how RFID tags on the bags of coffee simplified inventory control for the manufacturer, the warehouse, and the retailer. If the proponents of RFID have their way, every individual item you purchase, right down to individual cans of Dr. Pepper in a case, will have a unique RFID identifier. Some foresters are using RFID chips to identify standing timber for later harvest, and to track logs from the woods to the sawmill. Pretty much any item you purchase could carry an RFID tag, and the more expensive the item the greater the chance that it **will** have a chip somewhere on or in it. Most major electronic equipment is tagged, making it easy to determine if the equipment is still under warranty by verifying when the item was sold. The military makes extensive use of RFID technology to track everything from individual articles of clothing all the way to the location and deployment of tanks and airplanes. (There is a rumor that the military is also implanting RFID chips in the arms, legs, head, and torso of soldiers to aid in identifying and reconstructing their body should they be dismembered.)

In addition to simply tracking inventory, RFID technology allows companies like Walmart to practice Just In Time (JIT) ordering. That means that when the computer system detects that the inventory count for a particular item is getting low, the system itself can generate an order to the supplier. In addition, the system keeps track of the delivery time for that product. That way the system places orders for goods Just In Time to prevent the store from running out of that product. This same technology allows manufacturing plants to keep raw materials coming in just fast enough to keep production at peak rates. The advantage to the company using JIT ordering, of course, is that they don't have to maintain a large inventory of parts or materials, saving the company both money and space.

LOSS PREVENTION

Loss prevention and control is even more important than tracking inventory for many companies. The biggest culprit is usually *shrinkage*, or loss from shoplifting and, unfortunately, most commonly due to employee theft. Shrinkage refers to inventory reduction that isn't accounted for by sales. Items that are shoplifted leave the inventory but don't go through the registers so the inventory shrinks with no increase in revenue and no records. One local store put RFID tags on all of the medium- and high-priced items. They also put RFID readers at all store exits. This research showed that far more stolen inventory was leaving through the rear of the store. Once employees were told about the readers, shrinkage slowed significantly but didn't disappear completely. The managers were baffled. The shoplifted inventory cataloged by the RFID readers on the doors didn't account for the amount of missing inventory. Then they noticed that there was no reader on the chute used to pass recyclable cardboard out of the store. When they installed a reader on that chute, they found that some employees were placing high value inventory into boxes to be recycled. Their co-conspirators, working outside the store, were retrieving the items before the boxes were baled for recycling. By employing RFID readers, this store was able to reduce shrinkage by nearly 90%. Of course this same technology can be used to detect and catch non-employee shoplifters.

ACCESS

We briefly looked at the way RFID technology can be used to speed up your commute. RFID toll tags eliminate the hassle of stopping to pay tolls on a toll road. That is only one place these chips are commonly used to allow access. Some amusement parks, like the Disney theme park in Orlando, Florida give users tickets or bracelets with embedded RFID chips. Each ride has a chip reader, so the guest's whole experience can be monitored without the guest ever having to physically show their tickets. In addition, the bracelets on children are tracked so if a child becomes lost, the system can easily and quickly reunite the child with his/her family. The readers can scan and read the chip through normal clothing so the ticket can stay in the guest's pocket from the front gate throughout the park.

Automobile access is another valuable way RFID is being deployed. Many of the cars built since 1994 have an RFID reader built into the steering column. This reader looks for the specific ID code from a transponder built into the car's key. If that ID isn't present, the car simply won't start. For example, the newer Mini Coopers have a start button instead of a key and lock on the steering column. When the driver enters the vehicle, the RFID reader detects the presence of the chip in the key and enables the button. Industry experts estimate that this technology has caused a 50% reduction in automobile theft in Europe.

RFID technology can not only give you access to buildings, cars, and the like, they can also simplify the process of entering a country! If you have recently gotten a passport from the United States, any of the European Union countries, or many other countries, that passport contains an RFID chip. Exactly what is stored on the chip varies from country to country. Most European Union passports contain a wealth of personal information. Those data include name, date of birth, and even scans of the owner's fingerprints and photo. On the other hand, the chip on the U. S. passport only contains a reference number that identifies a file that contains the citizen's necessary passport control data.

PAYMENT SYSTEMS

RFID technology is most likely changing your day to day habits with regards to payment. As you saw in the development of RFID, Exxon was an early adopter of this technology with their "Speedpass." If you have one of the Speedpass keychain fobs, all you need to do to pay for your gasoline is wave the little black wand-like dongle near the payment area of the pump. When you finish pumping your fuel, Exxon charges the credit card associated with your Speedpass . You don't have to dig out your wallet, you don't have to find your credit card, and you don't have to enter your zip code or other identifying data. Life is easy.

Dongle

©Kendall Hunt Publishing Company

Figure 3   An artist's rendering of a dongle like the Speed Pass Dongle that we aren't allowed to show in the book.

The same principle applies when you use a toll tag. You zip along down the road, passing under the toll tag readers, never slowing down, not having to worry that you have the correct change, and your toll tag account is automatically debited. This is such a lucrative system for the toll road owners that many toll roads have completely done away with toll booths. If you don't have a toll tag, the camera system associated with the readers takes a picture of your car, capturing your license plate. Then the company sends you a bill for your toll charges. In most cases, the charge for using the toll road without a tag is higher, at times substantially higher, than the charge would be if you had a toll tag. This higher charge, sometimes two or three times the tagged charge, is supposed to act as an incentive to encourage you to get a tag! Using RFID technology makes your drive more pleasant, makes your commute shorter, and makes the toll road association more money. Remember, they get paid for people passing toll tag readers (I can't call them tool booths anymore).

Many of the major credit cards are now "chipped." You can simply wave your card **near** a card reader instead of the hassle of swiping it through the magnetic strip reader. That makes it faster and more convenient for you to check out. Some of the cards, coupled with specialized readers, can even read the card while it is in your wallet or purse so you don't even have to find and manipulate them.

As you can see, RFID technologies have integrated into almost all levels of our daily lives. And so far we have looked at the ways they make our lives easier, or at least more convenient. But as we have seen over and over, while the technologies are neutral, the uses and abuses to which they can be put are sometimes less than ideal. That is certainly the case with RFID.

THE DARK SIDE OF RFID

Probably no modern technology has generated more discussion, more outrage, more concern than RFID. In addition, no technology, except perhaps social media, poses such a major threat to your security and privacy. A large cohort of scientists, privacy experts, and security specialists have published numerous books, papers, and articles warning about the extreme dangers of this technology. Unfortunately, there is no way to address all of the concerns these experts have raised and keep the length of this section of the book reasonable. Therefore, I have limited this discussion to some of the most common and dangerous offenders. If you are interested, or worried about this technology, I suggest you start by reading the excellent book, Spy Chips by Katherine Albrecht. It was published in 2005, and after you read it you can just imagine how far things have come in the decade since it was published. I will warn you, you won't look at RFID the same way after reading her book. In addition, if you Google "RFID dangers" you will find over 250,000 articles. So what has these eminent researchers so concerned? Let's take a look.

LITTLE CHIP IS WATCHING

Well, actually, readers are watching the little chip, but those chips can be used to track you within a store, or down the street, or even right inside your house. Criminals can purchase an RFID tag reader for the imposing sum of $8.00 on eBay. That reader allows them to scan you and your purchases to see if you are worth robbing. Readers, mounted along most any route you could take, can track you using the chips in your clothing, credit cards, personal identification documents, etc. With some small effort, a couple of people could track everything you do, everywhere you go, and almost everything you purchase. Loyalty cards with embedded RFID chips allow the store to track you as you shop. Cameras tied to the readers watch you and record how long you spend looking at a particular items, whether you return any items, etc. Your whole shopping experience can be cataloged and then sold to a *data miner.* These folks compile data about individual consumers and then sell the results of those compilations to anyone who wants to find out about you. And, not only do these miners report what you have done, they are also frighteningly good at predicting what you are going to do! They can predict, with great accuracy, what you will buy in the grocery store, what type of car you will buy, etc. One example of the results of data mining becomes obvious in the fall, during football season. Data miners have discovered that people often buy disposable diapers and beer in the same trip to the store. To facilitate that, many stores will put a display of beer next to or near their diapers. Although, it is practically impossible to rid yourself of all of these sneaky little spies, in the next few pages we will examine some methods that may be used to possibly disable at least some of the chips that pose a threat to you.

CREDIT/DEBIT CARDS (SPENDING MADE EASY)

RFID embedded in credit cards leads to greater spending (first they wanted to do away with cash, so we would all use digital currency, but researchers found that even the typical credit/debit card transaction took too long, and provided opportunities for the customer to change his/her mind and halt the process of checking out). Why is this important? There are two, distinctly different reasons this technology has been implemented.

First, retailers discovered that when people use cash, and actually feel the money leaving their hands, customers tend to be more frugal. When you see, and feel, those dollars leaving your hand, it is a more personal and profound experience than if you just swipe a plastic card. If you spend $100 on groceries, handing over ten $10.00 bills is a lot different than swiping a little plastic card and signing your name. Somehow the plastic card doesn't really represent your hard earned dollars so it is easier to spend them. But having to swipe your card and sign your name involves more thought than just having the money automatically deducted from your account. So when your card has embedded RFID technology you don't even have to swipe and sign, the only thing that indicates you how much money you have spent is the receipt, which you handily ignore when the clerk hands it to you. This "improvement" in the payment system is designed to help you spend the maximum amount of money with the least thought. It's great for the merchant, but possibly not so great for your budget.

Having RFID tagged merchandise is another place where this technology speeds your spending. Back in the old days, the ancient days, when dinosaurs roamed the earth, the person running the cash register manually keyed in the price of each item you bought. To speed up the process, the bar code and bar code reader were deployed. This made separating you from your money a more efficient process. Instead of keying in each price, all the checker needed to do was pass the item's barcode past a reader and the register would automatically record the price. (This also made the job of running a cash register much simpler.) RFID makes it even faster. You could push your loaded cart past an RFID reader and nearly instantly (well, in a few microseconds) the system would recognize each of the chips on the items. Then the system would deduct the amount you spent using the RFID chip in your credit card. You could just keep walking out to your car, no need to stop, no need to wait for someone to total your bill, it will all be done instantly and automatically. You won't even see how much you spent unless you bother to look at your credit/debit card statement at the end of the month.

That sounds really convenient, doesn't it? And it is wonderful for the merchant. But let's look at what happens when you leave the store. As you walk across the parking lot, someone could scan your cart and know exactly what you have in it. You see, those RFID tags don't go dormant when you leave the store. When individual item tagging was first introduced, the manufacturers explained that the chips had to be within 18 inches of the reader. They claimed that the chips couldn't be read beyond that. Unfortunately, hackers quickly proved that those RFID tags could be read up to 35 feet away! Some RFID tags can be read MILES away. It all depends on the type of tag, and the power of the reader. So let's say you buy a really cool new television. It has all the latest features, and it's your pride and joy. Of course that television has an RFID chip somewhere in or on it. If a thief were looking for a valuable television to steal, he or she could drive up and down your street scanning for expensive television sets using a PC and an RFID reader. If your television is sitting within 35 or so feet of the street, the thief could see exactly what you own and get a good idea of where it is in your home. At the same time, the thief could use RFID data to see if you had anything else worth stealing. "Ah," you say, "I'll just disable or remove the RFID tag." That's a great idea, except doing that, if you can even locate the tag, will void your warranty! Many items have the RFID chip actually embedded within the body or case. Now, let's take this scenario to the next level. Suppose someone wanted to monitor your consumption of, say, alcohol. All they would need do is either scan your home, and record all of the bottles and cans of alcohol, or even more simply, just scan your garbage and recycling to see what you threw out. They could do this with a good RFID reader, without ever even slowing down as they passed your house.

And it's not only your home that presents such a delightful target for snooping. You can be tracked by someone just by following the RFID chips in your clothing, shoes, etc. Much of the clothing in our country has RFID tags actually woven into the fabric of the article. One extremely disgusting example will suffice. If you or your lady friend wear Victoria's Secret "Angel Fantasies" lingerie anyone with a decent RFID tag reader and a PC can scan the tags in the garments she is wearing as she walks by and know not only the name of the item, but the size and color as well. They can even pull up a picture of the item on their PC. This is an extremely vulgar violation of her privacy and extremely creepy as well.

What about the tags in our passports? Supposedly if you keep your passport tightly closed, the RFID chip is protected from being read. But if the passport is even slightly open a good reader can capture the data on the chip. On U.S. passports, those data consists of only a reference number into a file maintained by the Immigration Department. On the other hand, European passports chips contain personal data like the owner's picture, fingerprints, identification number, etc. One real concern with chipped passports is not that a bad actor can steal information from them, but rather that they can identify you and the country you come from at a distance. Remember, it's possible to read a passport chip at a distance. Suppose a terrorist wanted to harm people from the United States. That terrorist could build a bomb with an RFID reader as the trigger. When someone carrying a U.S. passport walked past the bomb, it would recognize the U.S. passport tag, and detonate. That is, unfortunately, not fiction. There is an older YouTube video that shows how this could work. The video explains how even a slightly open chipped passport is vulnerable to being read at a distance. The URL of the video is: https://www.youtube.com/watch?v=-XXaqraF7pI

One of the most controversial applications of RFID technologies involves implanting these chips in people. Proponents argue that if your identifying data are on a chip embedded in your arm, you could never lose it, have it stolen (unless they stole your arm, too), or forget to bring it with you. Some companies like CityWatcher.com give their employees the option of having a chip implanted in their arm instead of carrying a chipped card. That chip provides access to highly restricted areas of the company. If an employee doesn't want to be implanted, they are given an ID card with the RFID chip in it. Something to consider is what happens when an employee leaves the company? Do they dig out the chip? Another argument for this technology is in the medical field. If you had a chip implanted in your arm that contained your medical information the chip would give doctors access to your medical records and allergies even if you were unable to communicate. That way the doctors could do a better job of treating you since they would know your medical history. Of course, anyone else who read the chip would have access to those data as well. As noted above, a good application of this technology employs an active RFID chip to track, find, and monitor a wandering elder individual. On the other hand, that same technology can function as a terrible violation of privacy when implanted in people without special needs. Even a passive chip, like the chip used to identify your puppy, if embedded in a person can be a severe privacy violation, since the chip could enable someone with malicious intent to track the "wearer."

Any document that contains an RFID chip is vulnerable to being copied. In one case, an RFID researcher drove around San Francisco with an RFID reader in his car. In just 20 minutes he was able to capture and clone (copy) 4 drivers' licenses and passports! Suppose someone with that sort of equipment set up in an airport? They could capture dozens if not hundreds of IDs! So while that little RFID chip in your passport makes going through immigration easier, and might be a more absolute way to identify you, it also makes you very vulnerable to identity theft. Any documents, including cards, drivers licenses, passports, etc. that contain an RFID chip can be read and copied from a distance. Just how far depends upon the power of the reader and the quality of the antenna attached to the reader. As the San Francisco example illustrates, if that distance is at least 10-15 feet it is far enough that you won't know if your document is being scanned and your information copied.

Identity theft and privacy violations are at the heart of the concern with the rapid and pervasive spread of this technology. From being tracked using the RFID chips in your clothing to following your car via your toll tag, the potential for abuse of this form of identification is frightening. I'm sure you can see from the few examples listed above how this technology can be used to surveil you, itemize and enumerate your possessions, and create situations where individuals with less than honorable intentions can use the tags on the objects in your possession to mark you as a potential victim. Consider the situation where an individual is wearing three or four items of clothing that each contain a chip. In addition, they are carrying a couple of credit cards that are chipped, and their driver's license is chipped as well. With just one pass of an RFID reader, a bad actor can identify and track their target even in a crowd. With the right hardware, that malicious individual could even reprogram certain types of RFID chips to deny the legitimate user access to their possessions and accounts! The world of RFID is rife with opportunities to bring harm to users. On top of all these other threats, RFID technology in documents makes it very simple to steal your identity. So what can you do to protect yourself?

FOILING THE RFID ATTACKER

Obviously, the best way to prevent malicious individuals from stealing your data is to avoid having any RFID chips. That means not participating in stores' "loyalty programs," not having a credit card that contains a chip, and not buying anything that contains a chip. Unfortunately, that is becoming nearly impossible to do! Most credit card companies are now replacing older cards with RFID embedded ones. And most stores now have RFID credit card readers because the government dictated that if a store does not use the new RFID cards they are vulnerable to credit card fraud. In the past, if a store was victim of credit card fraud, the issuing bank would reimburse the store for their loss. Now however, if a store suffers a fraudulent charge and they don't have the new reader, they are not reimbursed! As you have seen, RFID chips are pretty much ubiquitous, so avoiding them gets more difficult every day.

When you are dealing with identification documents that contain an RFID chip, the easiest way to protect the chip is to enclose the document in an RFID-blocking container. For example, for less than ten dollars you can purchase 10 or 12 RFID blocking sleeves for your credit cards and driver's licenses, as well as a couple of sleeves that can protect your passport. It is a little more hassle when you want to use a card because you will first need to remove it from the sleeve, but that is a small price to pay to keep your identity and bank account safe. Of course that won't work for things like the Spedpass, toll tags, clothing, or large items you purchase, like your television. But at least you can protect your documents. You can even use the low-tech solution of simply wrapping your RFID tagged documents in aluminum foil, which is supposed to block the RFID signals. However, I wouldn't recommend making yourself an aluminum foil hat, it won't help, and could actually amplify the evil, alien radio waves!

Well, how can you "kill" and RFID chip? First off, let me explain that while there are methods for "fixing" RFID tags so that they can't be read "accidentally," or even damaging then so they no longer function all the methods involve some risk. Some of the methods are fairly simple, others involve a bit more hardware, and pretty much all of them involve physical access to the item containing the chip. Each method is also dependent upon the placement of the chip, and the composition of the item containing the chip. For example, you can disable an RFID chip by microwaving it. However, if you microwave your Victoria's Secret delicate under-things, you will probably disable the chip, but you will also probably set your clothing on fire! That isn't the outcome most of us would choose.

A strong word of caution: It is illegal to modify or alter your passport in any way. It is illegal to tamper in any way with the chip in your passport. Do not attempt to disable the RFID chip in your passport. There are only two reasonable solutions to protect the chip in your passport. First, find a way to keep the cover tightly closed until you need to present it. The government claims that the cover of the passport will prevent the chip from being read if it is tightly closed. For example, put a couple of rubber bands around it to hold it shut. Second, you can place it in some sort of container, like the sleeves mentioned above that blocks any attempt to read it. There are some pretty fancy RFID blocking passport wallets available, and just a sleeve like those mentioned above will work just fine. Do not, under any circumstances attempt to modify your passport!

RFID tags can be permanently disabled by exposing them to microwave radiation for a few seconds. That works because the chip uses electromagnetic energy to power the circuit, and a microwave generates such a powerful signal, outputting so much electromagnetic energy that the chip is literally "burned out." The problem with this method is that it can also set fire to the item containing the chip! So as we mentioned above, you wouldn't want to put your Victoria's Secret lingerie in a microwave because you would most likely set them on fire. You couldn't put your television in the microwave, and even if you could, the microwave radiation could also fry all of the circuits in the TV!

However, most of these methodologies only work if you can locate the tag! You can purchase devices that locate RFID tags on eBay, or even on Amazon. Or, you can find plans to build one yourself. These devices work by putting out a small signal, and reading the returned signal. You move the device over the object in question until you get a strong signal back. Then you can carefully examine the item and attempt to locate the tag. Sometimes the RFID chip is located on a small tag, like the tag for washing instructions sewn into the garment. In other cases the tag is literally crafted into the garment itself. In hard goods, the tag may be molded into the plastic of the case, glued somewhere inside the case, or hidden somewhere else in or on the item. In some bottled drinks and such, the tag is actually in the cap. There are a lot of sneaky places to hide the RFID tag, and in a lot of cases, the manufactures don't make it easy to find. It's almost like the manufactures realized that some of us would try to find and disable those tags, so they tucked them into hidden spaces. Once you...finally...locate the tag you can attempt to disable it.

There are generally three different methods you can use to disable and RFID tag. (Remember, however, that if you disable the tag on an item with a warranty, you will most likely void that warranty. Please also remember that you must NEVER disable or in any way modify your passport!!!)

The first and easiest way to disable tags in documents is to place them into an RFID proof container. While this doesn't remove the tag, it prevents unauthorized individuals from reading or programming the tag. The most common method is to just put the document in an RFID proof sleeve or wallet. This is the ONLY legal way to prevent unauthorized access to your passport.

The next two methods of dealing with RFID tags is permanent. You need to physically alter the RFID tag. If the device is large enough, and accessible, simply cutting the trace or copper foil pathway where it attaches to the actual chip will disable it. This prevents the chip from receiving sufficient power to broadcast its data. It also prevents the chip from using the antenna to broadcast if it does obtain sufficient power.

The third, and usually most difficult way to disable an RFID chip is to burn it out. One way to do this, of course, is to microwave the item. We have discussed the risks associated with this methodology already. A more controlled way to "fry" the chip is to generate a local EMP (ElectroMagnetic Pulse.) This destroys the chip and usually presents much less risk to the item containing it. I am not going to tell you how to build an EMP "gun" but you can find detailed plans on Google and on YouTube. Please remember that if you generate an EMP, ALL electronics in the area around the generator may be damaged. One of the more common designs for an EMP generating circuit uses the electronics in a disposable camera. Again, remember that if you damage the RFID tag in some items you will void the warranty. **And finally, I need to say one more time, you MUST NOT alter your passport in any way!**

GLOSSARY

Term	Definition
Active RFID Tag	This type of tag contains a power source, usually a small battery or capacitor, and broadcasts its data either continuously or intermittently. This type of tag is most often used to follow moving objects, either animate or inanimate. For example, this type of tag is used to track the migration routes of several species of whale. Each time the whale surfaces, the tag sends location, temperature, and other environmental data to an orbiting satellite. The lifespan of these chips is a significant problem. They only broadcast as long as the power supply holds out. Of course the more often they broadcast, the more quickly they use up their power. Some of the more advanced chips can be recharged by induction so the chip itself can remain embedded.
Data miner	The business of data mining involves scanning many databases and other sources of data like store loyalty records collecting data on individuals. From all those data sources the data miner then can compile a comprehensive and frighteningly accurate picture of you, your spending habits, and your lifestyle. Data miners then sell the compilation of these data to people who want to advertise to you, or people who are doing background checks on you. The data collected, and the trends they show are called a predictive perspective. What that means is that the data miner can not only describe what you have done, but in many cases predict, with great accuracy, what you are going to do! Spooky indeed!!

Term	Definition
Passive RFID Tag	A passive RFID tag depends upon the reader to energize the chip. Exposing the antenna to radio waves of the correct frequencies causes electricity to flow to the chip. When the chip is activated in this manner, it broadcasts stored data back to the reader. These chips have an almost unlimited life span because they receive their energy from the external radio transmitter. The chips in your pets, and those used for inventory control are good examples of passive RFID tags.
Resonant frequency	The frequency at which a given molecule, or any other substance naturally vibrates easily. For example, glass has resonant frequencies between 1000 and 10,000 vibrations per second depending upon the composition of the glass and the size and shape of the glass object. Resonant frequency is easily demonstrated by running a wet finger tip around the rim of a partially full wine glass. At a specific speed, your finger tip will vibrate as it slides along the glass. When you reach the resonant frequency of that particular glass, it will begin to "sing." There are examples of people playing these glass instruments on YouTube. Another example is the annoying buzz or hum that emanates from your dashboard when you reach a certain speed. What's happening is the vibrations of the tires on the pavement match the resonant frequency of something in your dashboard, causing it to vibrate as well. Another term for this phenomenon is "harmonics". To see this in action, Google "Tacoma Narrows Bridge Collapse." That is one of the most famous instances of resonant frequency destroying a huge structure.
Shrinkage	This term refers to inventory reduction that isn't accounted for by sales or disposal of the items. Items that are shoplifted leave the inventory but don't go through the registers so the inventory shrinks with no increase in revenue and no record of where the item(s) went. Unfortunately, for most stores the most common and most expensive cause of shrinkage is employee theft.
Transponder	In general, a transponder is a device that receives a radio signal, and then broadcasts a reply signal that is different than the signal received. One of the common uses for this technology is the IFF transponder in airplanes that allows a RADAR operator identify the plane. Transponders can be either active or passive. An active transponder has an on board power source and is capable of transmitting data at a significant distance. On the other hand, a passive transponder only replies when it is energized by an incoming radio wave.

The Deep Web and the Dark Net

Loosely defined, the *Deep Web* is the portion of the Internet left inaccessible to the standard search engines, (Google/ IXquick/ Yahoo/ DuckDuckGo, etc). It's composed of servers that are set up so they cannot be indexed by the standard search engine spiders, so the content never shows up in those searches. Most of these are the databases that require you to enter a specific set of search terms into a specialized search engine.

The second term we need to address is the *Surface Web*. That describes the data and Websites that ARE available using the standard Web search engines. Another name for this part of the Internet is the *Clearnet* because none of the contents are encrypted. That part of the Internet that you normally use is the Surface Web. However, most people use part of the Deep Web on a daily basis as well. The content behind a paywall (Netflix, Hulu), and content like online banking/email/anything with an encrypted login would be, by the previous definition, part of the Deep Web. While you don't need specialized software, other than your browser, to access the Surface Web, stepping into the Deep Web requires specialized search engines.

The third term that comes into play when talking of the Internet is the *Dark Net*. That is a small part of the Deep Web with even more restricted access. It is the home of some of the more questionable web content, and is used for specialized functions, some of which may be nefarious. The correct, read that technical or geeky, term for the Dark Net is "Tor's Hidden Services." Many people, and most media, like newspapers, Websites, and blogs often confuse the Deep Web with the Dark Net. The vast majority of the data on the Deep Web is simply highly specialized and of interest to a limited number of people. In this section we will first look at the Deep Web, because that is composed of sites that most of us use whether we are aware of it or not. Next we will address the Dark Net.

The standard image of the three parts of the Internet is an iceberg, it looks something like this:

As you can see from Figure 1, the vast majority of the data and information on the Internet is in the Deep Web not the Surface Web. Estimates on the content and size of the Deep Web range from 100 to 1000 times as much data as that in the Surface Web. The Deep Web is HUGE! One reason there isn't a concrete value for the size of the Deep Web is simply because there isn't any really good way to search and catalog it as a whole. In addition, the Deep Web is constantly growing and changing, so a measurement of the size today would be out of date by

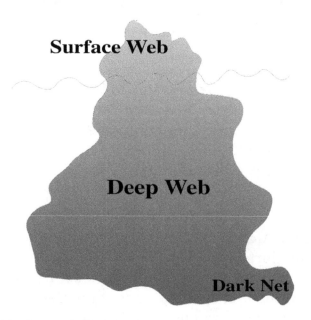

Figure 1 The Internet viewed as an iceberg

tomorrow. There are some companies that are attempting to do just that, but so far the vastness of the Deep Web has eluded their best efforts.

So how do you search the Surface Web? The searching is going on all the time, and as web sites change and add content, the search engines keep updating their databases to reflect the changes. A *spider* or *web crawler*, is specialized program that roams the Internet, going from link to link, landing on sites, usually Web pages, and recording the key words used to identify that site. Then the spider reports the Internet Protocol (IP) address (and, usually, the domain name) and keywords from that site back to the search engine that sent it out. Those data, the keywords and IP address, make up the database that the search engine searches. Most Websites are visited at least daily by one or more spiders. It is possible to put special file of instructions at the beginning of the first page of a site to tell spiders NOT to report back any data on that site or portions thereof. In that case the site (or parts of it) will be invisible to the common search engines. (It will not be part of the Surface Web.) On the other hand, it is possible to code a series of keywords on the first page of a site, and the spider will use those keywords in its report. If neither of those special codes are present, the spider will usually look at the first few paragraphs of the first page looking for what appear to be important terms. Those terms will be the keywords the spider reports back to the search engine. However, if the data on a server can only be accessed by a specialized search engine, they too will remain "hidden." Those data and the sites that host them comprise the Deep Web.

A little background here. When you enter a search term into a search engine, let's say Google, the software searches the Google database and reports back the addresses of pages that contain one or more of the terms you are searching for.

That database is constantly being updated by data returned by the spiders. We will look at the format of a search engine request in a bit. The search engine does not actually go out into the Internet at the time of your search. Rather, it simply searches the database built by its spiders. That is why you can get search results that are inaccurate, or be directed to sites that no longer exist. But if a site isn't in the search engine's database, it effectively doesn't exist on the Surface Web, and so it is considered part of the Deep Web.

Search engines use some special, magical, terms to build the string they use to search their database. Here are a few tips that will make your Internet searches more efficient and productive:

- Use at least 5 terms in your search, more are better. Since the Web contains millions of sites, if you just have one or two terms in your search the number of sites returned will be tremendous and the odds of finding exactly what you want will be difficult and time consuming. Instead, put as many terms as you can think of in your search string. That will help the search engine refine the results and give you a more manageable number of results. If you type in the phrase Christmas store Michigan, the search engine will give you all the sites that contain the words Christmas AND store AND Michigan. A bit over 43 million results! The sites with all of those words as key words will show up first. If you type in the string Christmas store Frankenmuth Michigan your search will only return 72 thousand results. That is quite a bit better.

- Use the magic of asterisk (*). To expand your search, often expanding it to amazing levels, you can use the asterisk between two words and you will get everything that has those two words with anything between them. For example if you were to search for Christmas * store your returned results would contain any site containing those two words as boundaries with any number of words between them. Like, Christmas is a time when I visit the toy store. Use the asterisk to get ideas to refine your search.

- But suppose you want to search for an exact phrase? Let's say you want to search for the phrase Your mother was a hamster and your father smelt of elderberries. You don't want all the sites that talked about hamsters or fathers or elderberries, you just want that one phrase. The trick is to put the phrase in quotation marks. "Your mother was a hamster and your father smelt of elderberries" will only return links to sites with those exact words in that specific order.

- You can use the OR operator to expand your search. This is especially valuable if you want to search for two or more phrases. For example, you could search for "Telford Tanager" OR "Torrid Tales of Technology" and you would get any site that addressed either of those two terms as well as those that had both. Again, using OR will expand your set of results.

- Use the NOT or minus (-) operator to restrict your results. For example, if you wanted to see sites that talked about "Torrid Tales of Technology" but not about Telford, you could enter the search string: "Torrid Tales of Technology" -Telford and the search engine wouldn't return any sites that contained Telford's name.

Use those tips and you might just find what you are looking for a wee bit faster.

The majority of the data on the Deep Web are accessible you if you know the "trick." You just need to use the specialized search software provided by the website/database you are visiting. The Deep Web is made up of databases like those of private companies, universities, government entities, and other sources that want to keep their data private, only accessible to a select group of people, or only accessible using their search engine. For example, a company may have a human relations database. In that database are company policies, employment data, salary schedules, and the like. The company has no need or wish to share those data with the whole wide world, so they restrict access to their own employees. They can do that either by using a VPN (Virtual Private Network), or specialized software designed to only search and access their database. A VPN can be set up such that only users logged into that private network are allowed access to specific databases. That is how my college works. If I am not logged onto a computer on one of the campuses, I won't be able to access much of the faculty database. And if I am on campus, I must use the search tools that database provides to access those data. Databases that restrict access like that are part of the Deep Web. Another example of Deep Web content is your local newspaper. Most newspapers allow access only if you go into the news database from their Web page. That allows them to confirm that only their subscribers are accessing their content. Estimates run as high as 95% of the content on the Deep Web is only available by using specialized search engines. As we have seen, the Deep Web is much larger than the Surface Web (that part of the Web accessible by common search engines). The one drawback is that you usually can't search a site until you actually access that site. In other words, you can't do a generic search you must use the site-specific search engine.

Here is a little exercise for you. Go to CNN.com or MSN.com. It's OK, go there now, and I'll be waiting for you when you get back. Once you get to one of those sites, click around on the site, using the links provided. You may only use your mouse, you may not type in anything. Review some of the day's news, maybe an advertisement or two, and then come back to me here. Again, I'll be patiently awaiting your return.

....

Welcome back! Let's look at just what you were just doing. Just by clicking on the links associated with the stories, you were retrieving data from the CNN news services database. However, you didn't need any special software to get to those data. All you needed was your handy dandy search engine to get to the site and a browser. You were playing on the Surface Web.

Now for your next assignment, go to Expedia.com or Priceline.com or some other travel Website. Once there, retrieve some data, *just using links like you did at CNN.* For example, find out the cost of an airline ticket from Houston, Texas to Chicago, Illinois leaving next Friday. You must find those data ONLY by clicking on links. You may NOT use the search tools provided on those sites. You may NOT touch your keyboard and enter ANY data. Go and try it, as before I'll be patiently awaiting your return.

.... hum de dum...hum de dum.....(little known fact, you can't hum with your nose plugged!)

Argggg! Oh Dear! You can't!!! Hmmmm. Guess what...those data are in the Deep Web. Therefore, results are not accessible by the standard search engines or by just clicking on a link. You must use the custom search engine built into that specific Website to access the data in those databases. So you see, the Deep Web has a lot of accessible data, but they are only accessible using specialized search tools like those on the travel Websites. Some estimates put the size of the Deep Web at over 900 billion pages. In contrast, the largest Surface Web database, Google, contains access to about 12 billion pages. For the most part, there is nothing especially scary about the Deep Web. The library at my college is part of the Deep Web. You can't search the library's collection directly from Google. To browse the library's collection you need to go the library's Website, and use the search engine there. Another example would be the Dallas County, Texas home page. There you can find all sorts of data about who owns property in the county, the court dockets, all kinds of amazing data. However, you must use the Dallas County search engine to retrieve those data. The thousands, (millions?), of records in those databases are only accessible through the search engines provided by the county. This is another example of data that are part of the Deep Web. Most people often use the Deep Web, they just don't know the name for it.

As I hope you have seen, the Deep Web is mostly just a whole bunch, a jolly great big whole bunch of data that are available only by using a specialized search engines that specifically target the database(s) you are interested in. Let's get a wee bit more specific. How would you find out how much an individual paid in property tax, in Tarrant County, Texas, last year? (Hint: Go to http://taxoffice.tarrantcounty.com/AccountSearch.asp). You can't get any data directly from that page, and you can't Google, "How much property tax did John Smithe pay," either. If you enter that search string, you will be given lots of links to different property tax sites in different counties. However, you will still need to use the specialized search tool available on each Website to actually retrieve the data. Once on the site, you will fill in the name of the individual you wish to inquire about and the Tarrant County search engine will retrieve the requested data.

The Deep Web also contains much of the data that were available prior to the explosion of the World Wide Web. Way back in the early 90s, some colleges offered courses in "Searching the Internet." Yup, there was an Internet before there was a World Wide Web. HTML (HyperText Markup Language), the code used to craft Web pages, was invented in 1990. It is a relatively recent addition to the Internet. So how did we search the Internet in PWWW (Pre-World Wide Web)? We used search engines that indexed particular groups of sites. The very first of those search engines was called Archie (short for Archive). It ran on Unix-based machines, and accessed files across the Internet on specific Archie servers. Remember, this was in the day of text only files! Here is a link you can use to try out the Archie search engine; http://archie.icm.edu.pl/archie-adv_eng.html. Note, this example of Archie resides on a server in Poland. Because this is an older machine, and it is searching the files it has not a database, the response time might be just a wee bit slow. Here is a screen shot of the Archie Web page. In this case, we are asking Archie to find information about Internet Security.

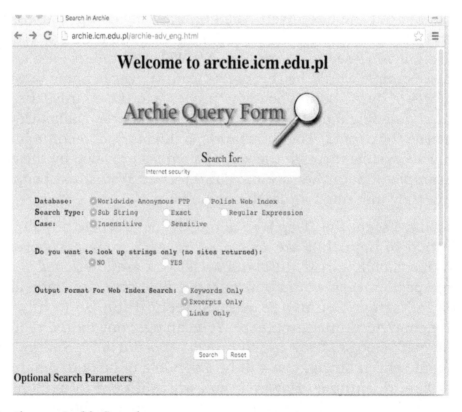

Figure 2   Starting an Archie Search

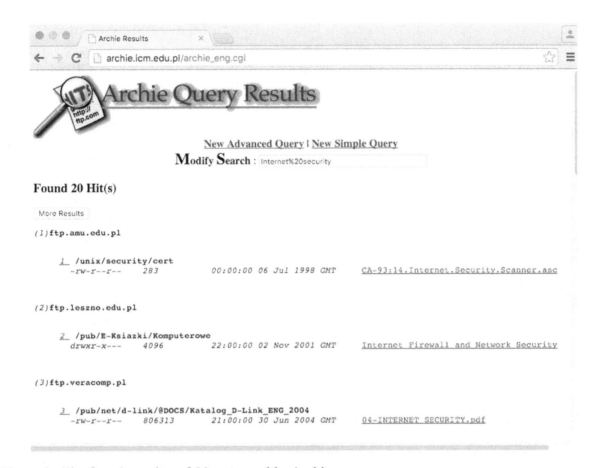

Figure 3   The first 3 results, of 20, returned by Archie

Again, remember that this server is located in Poland, and that particular Archie server may not have access to all the Archie databases in the US. It's important to note that in most cases, Archie only returns text data but as you can see from the Figure, it also returned a PDF document. How cool is that!

In addition to Archie, there were a number of other search engines/systems that contained different data. Veronica, JugHead, and Gopher were all popular search tools. Gopher is especially interesting in that it usually had the largest repository of information. It was a search tool developed by the University of Wisconsin (The Golden Gophers), hence its name. It was also a play on the term used to describe a new person, usually a lower level person, in an office environment. They are the 'go-fer' as in "go fer coffee" or "go fer the mail"...etc. The Gopher program accessed data files in many different data centers, called "Gopher holes." Yes, they sorta took that whole gopher thing and ran it into the ground. There are two important things about Gopher:

1. It provided a very powerful and wide-ranging search tool primarily used by academics. Of course, back in the 90s the majority of searches on the Net were academic in nature.

2. It allowed researchers to search a large number of files on a lot of sites to find the information they were looking for. And, with one search, it gave access to all of those data. That saved the researcher a lot of time since they didn't have to log into each server and search it individually.

Is there any way to retrieve data from the Deep Web without using specialized search engines? Well, there are several companies that have set up specialized search engines to do just that. One of them is BrightPlanet (www.BrightPlanet. com). They provide a service to large corporations and individuals to index many of the sites in the Deep Web to return data on specific content. They provide data to financial, healthcare, intelligence, and law enforcement organizations, among others. Their "product" is very different from the normal search engine. With Google, for example, you are given the URL (Uniform Resource Locator) of the Web pages that contain some or all of the terms you are searching for. Along with the URL you usually get a few lines of text that describe the site. It is up to you to actually go to that site and access the data. All too often, however, the search engine database is effected by "link rot." In other words, while the search engine thinks the page is there, it has disappeared and those data are lost or at best the URL has changed. With "data harvesting," a term Bright Planet uses, not only is the URL captured, but their search tool also collects (harvests) all of the content at that site. Google does something similar, with cached pages. They create a large data set containing all of the data on all of the sites of interest. Let's look at an example. Suppose you are really, deeply concerned about a particular political situation, say the protection of wolves in the west and south. Bright Planet has the ability to index every newspaper in the US, so they can build you a data set that contains all the newspaper articles written about wolves anywhere in the U.S., or just in the western states, for the length of time you specify. Remember, in most all cases the actual newspaper articles and located in the newspaper's site, which is in the Deep Web.

So that's what's available on the majority of the Web, either the Surface Web or the Deep Web. Now let's take a look at a fairly small, but notorious, corner of the Deep Web that takes even more specialized tools and knowledge to explore.

THE DARK CORNER OF THE DEEP WEB

A part of the Deep Web is referred to as the Dark Net. First of all, lots of folks confuse the Deep Web with the Dark Net. That isn't surprising because the Dark Net exists within the Deep Web; it is part of the Deep Web. Indeed, many of the articles about the Deep Web and the Dark Net either confuse the two, or worse, use the terms interchangeably. However the differences between the Surface and Deep Webs and the Dark Net are profound. While the first two, especially the Surface

Web are designed to make finding things easy, the Dark Net is most concerned with anonymity and privacy. There are no search engines that plumb the depths of the Dark Net and give you results across its many sites. The information in the Dark Net is designed to be accessed by those searchers who know exactly what they are looking for, and often even know exactly where to find it. It is a very private and personal place. There are sites that have links to other sites, but some of the links are broken, and some don't go to the same sites they initially accessed. And, of course, some of the links go to completely different sites than they seem to. The Dark Net is a fluid and ever-changing place.

It's not a good idea to access the Dark Net until you have put in place a number of safeguards. I strongly recommend that you do some serious research into accessing the Dark Net before you set foot, or cursor, in that perilous part of the Internet. Below I list the steps I have taken to prepare to venture into the Dark Net to do research for this book. To my mind, those are a minimal set of precautions. Please don't go "play" in the Dark Net without adequate preparation and a good idea of what you might well be getting into. The Dark Net is an amazing reference, a mind boggling mixture of different motives and material. But it is not a safe place to access unless you are prepared.

The most important aspect of the Dark Net is that it lets you be relatively anonymous. Unfortunately, several security holes in the Tor browser (modified version of Firefox) have been found which compromised anonymity. The most famous was a form of Javascript exploit. However, some are being patched as I write this. Anonymity is both a good and a bad thing. It is a great boon for individuals who value their privacy. There are several reasons you might want to be anonymous on the Net. You might be a whistle blower, and don't want to get fired, or worse, for "blowing the whistle" on your company on your government. Eric Snowden used the Dark Net to initially publish his famous reports on the NSA abuse of your privacy. You might be living in a country where the government is oppressive and retaliates against anyone who questions or criticizes it. You may be in an abusive relationship and need protection from your spouse or someone else who is abusing you. For some of us, it is as simple as wanting our communications be private. Not because we intend to do something illegal, but rather because we believe that all people have a fundamental right to privacy and anonymity. It's something like writing a letter and putting it in an envelope rather than writing the same information on a post card. A letter is supposed to be private, while anyone can read what you write on a postcard. Just because you want to be private and anonymous doesn't necessarily mean you are going to do something bad. In fact, much of the Dark Net traffic is made up of private conversations and blogs that have no illegal, unethical, or immoral intent. It's just conversations among individuals who value their privacy. The Dark Net is only accessible through the Tor network, and so provides the necessary anonymity to these folks. Through the

Dark Net they can learn about the rest of the world, let the rest of the world know what is happening in their country and/or to them. In addition, the Tor network and the Dark Net provide whistle blowers like Edward Snowden a relatively safe medium to let the world know what our government is up to. There are many, many good, safe, moral, ethical, responsible reasons why someone would want to use the Dark Net. They might be interested in doing research on just what is available. They might want to share confidential information that they feel should be made public without putting themselves at risk. They may just simply want to remain anonymous, and preserve their privacy. (I happen to think this is the very best reason of all!)

On the other hand, there are individuals who want to engage in some sort of nefarious activity, like selling drugs or weapons, and want to remain anonymous to avoid prosecution. (Remember, the technology is neutral, it's the use to which it's put that is either good or bad.) The Dark Net is such a deep topic, pun intended, that you will need to take several precautions before you venture into this realm. The following is just partial list of the precautions you must take. There is an excellent reference that goes into much more detail referenced the "References" section of this article.

Before I list the preparations I made before I entered the Dark Net, let me again say that it is not necessarily a safe nor benign place to visit. It can be dangerous. It can cause you problems. There are some residents of the Dark Net that do mean you harm. So, if you really want to go there, you must do your own research on what's required to do so safely. I will list the things I did, and so far I have been safe, I think. There is no guarantee that what I did will work for you. You need to do your own research, and as I have said elsewhere, **_cavaet scrutator_** (Let the searcher beware!)

My preparation:

1. Get a safe system to use:

    a. Dedicate one computer as your search computer, and use it for nothing else. Buy a cheap, older model or re-purpose one of you older computers.

    b. Install a safe operating system on this computer. Linux is a minimum, but I recommend one or more of the following.

        1. Qubes: http://thehackernews.com/2015/10/secure-operating-system.html

        2. Whonix: https://www.whonix.org/ (This is the one I use)

        3. Tails: https://www.deepdotweb.com/jolly-rogers-security-guide-for-beginners/pgp-tails-virtual-box/ (This is the one I am looking to move to.)

2. Securely shred any data on this machine that is associated with you. Don't use this machine to access ANYTHING except the Dark Net. Don't use it to do your banking, rent videos, go to PayPal, or even do standard Surface Web searches. Be sure to clean the hard drive completely before you install the operating system, then check it again after you install the secure OS. To shred your files you might consider:

   a. Windows: http://www.howtogeek.com/72130/ learn-how-to-securely-delete-files-in-windows/

   b. Linux: http://linoxide.com/security/delete-files-permanatly-linux/

   c. Mac: https://www.intego.com/mac-security-blog/ how-to-securely-empty-trash-in-os-x-el-capitan/

3. Secure your network:

   a. It is best to use a public network like you library, coffee shop, school, etc. That way you have no regular address associated with your information.

   b. To work from your home, (Note, I do NOT recommend doing this!!) Use an ethernet cable to connect your Dark Net machine to your modem, and shut down your wireless network. As an alternative, you can set up a second, hardwired-only network. You don't want your Dark Net computer to be able to access any of your other machines nor your network. Be sure to turn off WiFi on this computer as well.

4. Set up a VPN (Virtual Private Network) connection. You will need to choose the one that makes sense for you.

   a. http://www.thetop10bestvpn.com/

   b. http://geeksflame.com/best-and-top-free-vpn-services/

5. Use only a Tor browser. (Whonix or Tails will try to only use the Tor system)

6. Do some additional research! You really need to know what you are getting into before you start. Some interesting sites for research include:

   a. http://cryptorials.io/how-to-access-the-deep-web-or-darknet-a-beginners-guide/ (Note this article confuses Deep Web with Dark Net!)

   b. https://www.reddit.com/r/darknetmarketsnoobs

    c. http://www.fastcompany.com/3026989/an-up-to-date-laymans-guide-to-accessing-the-deep-web

    d. http://www.techlicious.com/blog/what-is-the-deep-web/

Wow, that's a lot of work! Yes it is!! You wouldn't head off into the Amazon jungle without making some serious preparations, would you? This is a similar type of adventure. You need to do your homework, make careful preparations, and go slowly. If you decide to venture into the Dark Net, I hope you enjoy yourself. Oh, and be careful!

There are also legal considerations to take into account. Some security specialists believe even downloading the software or researching the topic puts you on several close-watch lists, and coming across material on the Dark Net which is illegal in most countries is probably extremely easy, due to the nature of obfuscated links. If you do venture into the dark side of the Net, please think about what you are doing, and how it may be viewed if your research becomes known to the authorities.

To be a wee bit redundant.. These references below will take you to articles about the Dark Net, but they will not take you directly into the Dark Net. Before you decide to even step one foot into the Dark Net, please take the precautions listed in the first reference below. While the Dark Net is interesting, fascinating, and even compelling, it is a potentially dangerous place to visit. You never really know if somebody is watching over your shoulder, just waiting for you to step into a forbidden/illegal site. Some sites are even "honey pot" sites, sites set up by law enforcement to lure individuals who have nefarious intentions into revealing themselves. It is possible that just by visiting one of these sites, without doing anything directly illegal, your name, address, etc. could be captured by law enforcement much to your detriment. On the other hand, you could arouse the interest of some sort of Internet predator who could make your life miserable. The best bet is to trust your common sense and stay away from places that look to be questionable. At a minimum, if you decide that you need to explore this little corner of the Deep Web, please read the first reference to HiddenWiki. Then follow their guidelines explicitly and exactly before you venture into this fascinating, intriguing, and potentially scary and dangerous part of the Net. In the immortal words of the great Roman hacker, **_cavaet scrutator_** (Let the searcher beware)

Remember, I make no form of guarantee that you will be safe, even if you take the precautions I listed above. I wrote this section so that you won't accidentally or naively follow a link or decide to explore this part of the Net. If you decide to explore the Dark Net, you are on your own, and you must be willing to take the risks involved. Good luck and for heaven's sake, be VERY careful!!

GLOSSARY

Term	
Clearnet	The portion of the Internet that is unencrypted, open to most anyone, and therefore not very private or secure. Most people who use the Internet spend the vast majority of their time in this part. It takes special software and/or access and/or permission to access the other parts of the Internet.
Dark Net	That part of the Deep Web that is usually only accessible through the Tor Network or other types of ultra secure access. Most of the data are encrypted to preserve privacy. While there are illegal/immoral contents on the Dark Net, the majority of sites are small peer-to-peer or friend-to-friend sites. The Dark Net is also used by people who could be persecuted if their emails/posts/sites were available to the general public.
Deep Web	The portion of the Internet that is not available using standard search engines like Bing/IXquick/Google/DuckDuckGo. The vast majority of the Deep Web is highly specialized information that is of value to only a few users. Access to these data requires the use of a specialized search tool that creates a query (question) for that specific database. An online library card catalog is an example of Deep Web data.
Ip Address	The **I**nternet **P**rotocol address, or Internet address of a specific device connected to the Internet. Each device that connects directly to the Internet must have a unique IP address. An example of an IPv4 address is: 209.85.128.12 which happens to be the address of one of the Google machines. To be pedantic, there's a good chance that this IPv4 address actually routes to a cluster of load-balancing servers or similar.
Spider	A small software program that traverses the World Wide Web collecting and reporting information about Web pages. Each search engine has its own spiders that continuously add information to the search engine's database. In most cases, the information returned contains only the keywords associated with the site, and the IP address of the site.
Surface Web	The only part of the Internet that most users are aware of. These are the data/Websites available using the standard search engines, Yahoo/IXquick/DuckDuckGo/ Google. Most people never knowingly leave the surface Web. Yet anyone who uses any type of login service (email, Facebook, Skype, etc. are all venturing off of the Surface Web). Today, most people are unaware of how commonly they use the Deep Web. The Surface Web is part of the Clearnet, or the unencrypted portion of the Internet.

Term	
Tor	**T**he **O**nion **R**outer, is a series of networks that provide anonymity for users by masking their Internet addresses and encrypting all the data as it travels across the Network. The easiest way to access this network is to use the Tor Browser bundle. You can download that open source stool from the Net. I recommend going to the site: https://www.torproject.org/projects/torbrowser.html.en and reading the instructions there before you download and install your very own copy of the Tor browser and begin using it. Remember, the response time of this browser will be a bit longer than you might be used to. That's because it is sending all your requests through a number of servers to give you total anonymity.
Web Crawler	See "spider"

REFERENCES

Dark Net:

http://www.hiddenwiki.org/what-is-hidden-wiki.html ← Go here first, follow their suggestions!

https://www.quora.com/What-are-some-cool-deep-Internet-websites#!n=12

To get an idea of the kind of things that are available on the Dark Net, you can take a look at this page. You can access the page using your normal browser, but please remember that if you decide to visit one of the sites listed on this page, you will first need to install a copy of the Tor Browser.

http://the-hidden-wiki.com/

Note, this is a surface version of the Dark Net site, and will not let you access any other sites unless you are running the Tor browser. Please take all the precautions you think prudent before you actually begin poking around in any part of the Dark Net.

Another good reference for using Tor on the Dark Net can be found at: https://www.aswat.com/files/Want%20Tor%20to%20really%20work.pdf

Please read that .PDF as an additional resource before you venture into the Dark Net.

The Infamous
24 Hour Challenge

A colleague and friend of mine has been giving his students the opportunity to experience the Amazing 24-Hour Challenge for years. Now you, too, can experience the fun and excitement of this amazing adventure. At its heart, this is a very simple little challenge; all you need to do is refrain from using ANY digital device for a measured, consecutive 24 hours. Now what could be easier than that? All you have to do is NOT do something! First we will look at the rules for the project, and then he will explain why this project is so very important to you, to your family, and to your friends. Since I adopted this challenge a few years ago, many of my students have joined his and ended up making this challenge a regular part of their lives. Yup, it's that good!

RULES

1. You may not use a computer in any form. This includes PCs, smartphone, or any device that has digitally processed input or output.

2. You may not use any other device that has a computer built into it. Some of the many: microwaves, CD and DVD players, television sets, MP3 players, most radios, most gasoline pumps, some refrigerators, etc. If it has a digital display, um, err, it's DIGITAL!

3. You may not watch someone else use digital devices. For example you may not go to a club where there are TV sets and watch the TV in the reflection of your partner's glasses, in a mirror, etc. You must eliminate your exposure to digital devices for 24 hours.

4. You may not use your cell phone, smartphone, or a cordless phone. (Of course you may use any type of communication device in an emergency.) TURN OFF your phone. If you use your phone as an alarm clock, see point 10. I have had a student "restart" this project 3 times before she decided that she really had to turn her phone off!

5. You may not use another person as a secretary or helper. That is, you may not have another person hold or use your cell phone and/or relay messages for you. For 24 hours you have no cell phone, except in emergencies. The

same goes for any other technology, you can't ride in their car while they use the GPS to navigate for you. You can't use the Uber car service, either. No one can use any technology on your behalf.

6. If you wander into the presence of a digital device, you must leave that area at once. You can't use them, you can't watch somebody else use them, and you can't observe them from a distance.

7. Other devices that are explicitly prohibited:

   a. ATMs – get your money before hand, or use a bank teller.

   b. Computerized gas pumps since these have a digital display.

   c. Credit card transactions that involve using a computer, like digital signature pads or digital swipe devices.

   d. Debit cards...any debit card transaction. Period. They are ALL computer-based.

   e. RFID payment devices, like a "smart pass" for gasoline or a toll tag.

   f. Automated toll roads; if you must use a toll road, you must stop and pay with cash. If there is no way to pay with cash...well...pick a different route.

   g. If there is any question about it, DON'T use it! (Many washing machines and dryers now have a digital component as well, as do some stoves!)

8. As much as possible, do this on a normal day; no hunting or camping trips. NOTE: If your normal day involves work and work requires the use of computers, choose another day.

9. You must be sober, and conscious, you may sleep for eight hours and nap for one hour. No mind altering substances today, except for those explicitly prescribed to you by your physician. "Sober" means sober—blood alcohol level of 0.00—no drinking!

10. If you do use a digital device by "mistake," or break any of the other rules, no worries, your 24 hours starts over at that moment.

ALLOWED DIGITAL DEVICES

1. Any digital device you need to use for medical reasons. (Note: Withdrawal from Xbox, WoW, Minecraft, Pokemon Go, etc. is NOT a medical excuse!)

2. Cell phones. If you think you are in danger, turn on your phone and use it. However, feeling lonely, sad, or out of touch with friends is NOT dangerous!

3. You may use your car. Yes, I know, you car is most likely controlled by several digital devices, but you may drive it. (You may NOT use, toll tags, GPS, radar detector, CD player, radio, navigation systems, backup cameras, etc. Sing, drive the speed limit, use a map! You need to cover the display if your vehicle has a built-in display.

4. Church – many churches use digital projection as part of the service. You are encouraged to worship if you choose to have your 24-hour experience happen on your day of worship. You may NOT use an online bible, etc. however.

5. The heating/ AC system in your house. You can still heat/cool your home, but don't play with the settings during your experience, and do cover the display.

6. Home security systems. You may arm your home security system, and disarm it. That's all. If your security system has cameras, cover the screens. You may carry a mobile "panic button" and only use it if you are in a critical situation. Your safety comes first!

7. Some students have been confused between digital devices and devices that just use electricity. You may use any device that uses electricity, so long as it doesn't have a digital component.

RESULTS/REPORT

When you have completed your digital sabbath, you will need to make a report on the experience. The exact format of the report is up to you, but it must contain the following parts:

Heading

1. Your name, the date of your project, and the start / end times.

Preparation (20% of your grade)

2. Everything you did to prepare for your day. Examples include:

   a. Getting cold cuts and drinks for the ice chest (if your refrigerator is digital)

   b. Telling everyone, especially your parents and significant others, that you will be off the grid for the day

   c. Planning with friends/spouse to do interesting things

   d. Enlisting friends/spouse to join you in the experience (Misery loves company....LOL)

   e. Filling your car with gasoline

Diary/Experiences

(This is the longest part of the report: 50% of your grade)

3. Record each time you found yourself looking/reaching/thinking about a digital device. Each entry should have the following parts:

    a. The time you experienced it

    b. what "it" was (i.e. I was trying to find out what time it was)

    c. How you handled it

    d. What thoughts you had about that activity and your progress through the day in general

4. Things you did to fill your time. Each should have a start/end time.

5. Amazing and enlightening observations you made during the day. Or, depressing and terrible observations you made during the day.

Conclusions

(This is the most significant part of the report: 30% of your grade)

6. Explain your reactions to your observations and experiences. Describe, in as much detail as possible, what you went through, how you coped (or didn't cope) with digital withdrawal. This is also the place to explain what, if anything, you are going to do differently based upon your reactions to this day. Some of my students have:

    a. Discovered that not having the TV, cell phone, or mobile computer as distractions allowed them to have longer and better conversations with their friends/spouse. Since they liked that interaction, they decided to have a digital sabbath monthly or even weekly.

    b. Learned how much time digital devices steal from them, and how much they were able to get done without digital distractions.

    c. Saw how much other people rely on their digital devices, and how distracted and distanced they appeared.

    d. Found that having a family meal with no digital devices is much more interesting than a meal when everybody is focused on their phone/computer/tablet/TV/game/etc. Many have decreed the dining room table a digital-device-free zone. (This is how we do it in my house, too.)

    e. Became aware of how dependent they were on their digital devices to feel "connected" to the world, regardless of how many people were around them.

WHY IS THIS SUCH AN IMPORTANT THING TO DO?

Across many different media, radio, TV, and print writers despair that as a group we have become far too dependent upon our digital devices. Tech writers, scholars, even religious leaders now advocate combating digital addiction by freeing yourself from your devices. They propose differing degrees of exposure limitations for various lengths of time. Some advocate simply leaving your cell phone home for a day, and at the extreme others advise being totally digitally free for several months. If you Google "Digital Sabbath" you will find over five hundred and seventy thousand hits! Obviously this is a problem. Should you get brave, and Google "digital addiction," you will be shown a monstrous thirty-six MILLION entries! Yes, my dear reader, there is a problem. And it isn't trivial. According to CBS News, "Digital addiction may damage your brain," and according to makeuseof.com, "Extreme Digital Addiction is Destroying Kids' Lives Around the Globe,". Not only are many people concerned that we may be becoming addicted to the Net, there are already companies that provide treatment for digital addiction. For example, reSTART has a Website and several programs designed to help users break their digital addictions. There are numerous sites on the Net that have tests you can take to see if you are addicted to your tech. However, the easiest and most accurate test is to take the 24 hour adventure! You might well be surprised by what you find. Most of the students who have taken this challenge had big surprises!

REFERENCES

http://www.cbsnews.com/news/digital-addiction-may-damage-your-brain-study/

http://www.makeuseof.com/tag/extreme-digital-addiction-destroying-kids-lives-around-globe/

http://www.telegraph.co.uk/women/womens-life/11494737/Your-phone-is-ruining-your-life.-We-all-need-a-digital-sabbath.html

https://thedigitalsabbath.wordpress.com/introduction/

http://www.netaddictionrecovery.com/

http://www.nightingalehospital.co.uk/test/technology-addiction-test/

Sample 24 Hour Challenge Report
(This is a very well done report, it received an A.)

The following is a report submitted by one of my friend's students. She did an excellent job, and other than changing names to protect the innocent, the following are her exact words. This sample will give you an idea of how to approach the assignment, the level of detail needed to do a good job on the project, and the depth of thinking and examining your day that I expect in the conclusion. Note, you do NOT have to agree with this assessment, and if you found the experience less than enjoyable, feel free to express those thoughts, this is an excellent example due to the quality, not the conclusions.

Enjoy her day, I think you might just identify with some of the challenges she faced.

-------------------------------------- **Report starts here** --------------------------------------

A Very Good Student
Some day in some month in 2015

24 Hours Without Being Digital

Preparations: [BoyFriend] filled up his car the day before we began our no digital! We grabbed a cooler and filled it with ice and put water bottles inside, sandwich meat, cheese, lettuce, and dressings. We went out the night before and bought a bunch of chips and peanut butter and jelly. We were feeling a little fancy so we even bought some guacamole. I didn't tell any of my friends about the no digital thing, I only told my job just in case they tried to reach me. Haha

8:00 AM-	I just turned off my phone... It has begun :(
8:12 AM-	I am so used to always having my phone in my hand, it feels weird not carrying it with all around the house.
8:17 AM-	IT HASNT EVEN BEEN THIRTY MINUTES AND I WAS ALREADY LOOKING FOR MY PHONE TO CHECK THE TEMPERTURE! Oh boy, I wonder how today is going to go. When my phone dies I check it every 5 minutes for the time, forgetting EACH time that it is dead. I can't l'imagine 24 hours. I feel like a spoiled brat saying that. haha
8:34 AM-	I just told my mom what I'm doing and she actually really likes the idea. She said she won't watch TV when I'm home. I was expecting her to think that this was silly.

8:36 PM-   Here comes a day of eating nothing but sandwiches and chips. Yipee! Me and [BoyFriend] put everything in a cooler, I really hope the ice doesn't melt too soon. I've never really used one for longer than a couple hours.

9:21 AM-   I really don't want to be up this early! But the earlier I wake up, the earlier I can go to bed and the faster I can have my phone? I know I know, you like the way I think.

9:45 AM-   I'm having trouble using my watch, I kind of forgot how to read a regular watch. How sad is that? I'm having to sit here and count every little minute thing. Actually now that I think about it, I never really KNEW how to read them. I never had to actually use it because there are digital clocks everywhere and phones.

9:50 AM-   I think it is taking me longer to read the time than it is to actually get ready.

9:58 AM-   Getting ready without music on really SUCKS!

10:03 AM-   I REALLY NEED MY PANDORA RIGHT NOW!

10:08 AM-   So i'm getting ready and I cant find my hair spray, and I was looking for my phone to call my mom and ask her if she's seen it. WHY?!

10:15 AM-   Usually I can tell how long I have been getting ready for by how many songs have played, but I feel pretty lost

10:22 AM-   It's only been two hours and I already want my phone back.

10:35 AM-   I was just thinking about how long today is going to be. NO PHONE ALL DAY, WHAT? What am I going to do when I'm bored?

11:06 AM-   I just reached to check the time on my phone. DAMNIT! So it begins......

11:47 AM-   I honestly feel like a lost puppy dog without my phone. Come back to me! :'(It's not TOO bad right now because i'm keeping busy at school, but I know once I get home it will hit me harder.

11:55 AM-   I think the only hard thing for me today is not having my phone. I don't care about all the other things I can't use. I just want my phone back.

11:57 AM-   Is this really an addiction? How can I feel so different without my phone? haha

12:01 PM-   Once again I was looking for my phone to check the time. Why? I have a freaking watch on And I KNOW I can't use my phone today.

12:10 PM-	I'm <u>REALLY</u> not liking this whole "no phone" thing. I feel like i'm having withdrawals, as sad as that sounds. I feel antsy and useless. I never realized how much I actually use my phone, and depend on it. I DONT EVEN KNOW WHAT THE TEMPERATURE OUTSIDE IS!
12:11 PM-	I'm bored and I want to look at IFUNNY.
12:17 PM-	OMG! I just tried to grab my phone to check the time...AGAIN! This is going to be a LONGG day. How is it possible to forget so easily that I CANNOT USE MY PHONE?!
12:30 PM-	I feel like I'm going through a break up, haha. All I can think about is how I CANT use my phone.
12:32 PM-	I have a question I CANNOT find in my text book..I want to search it on my phone.. just once. PLEASE?!
12:34 PM-	Oh jeeze, I just remembered we have another car ride without music. So fun.
1:45 PM-	So I'm on my way home, and I'm not going to lie, this car ride WITHOUT music is really really AWFUL! I'm so hungry, but I already pre-planned my meals and NONE of it sounds good right now. Oh the struggles of living with no technology.
1:47 PM-	All I can hear is [BoyFriend]s loud turbo crap!
2:00 PM-	I just remembered and inside joke me and my friend have, and I was about to text it to her! This disappointment is endless. I think it is so strange that I keep forgetting this whole no phone thing. It is habit for me to be checking my phone every ten minutes, and texting people 24/7.
2:29 PM-	I got home and spent a good 20 minutes with my kitty cat, I think she really enjoyed all my attention. I wish it wasn't so cold outside or I would take my dogs on a walk. Maybe later, maybe.
2:36 PM-	I am so bored, its making me tired. I want to take a nap really bad but I KNOW I wont just magically wake up in an hour. What to do, What to do! I guess ill play with my doggies.
2:39 PM-	So bored.... what would people do back in the day? I wish I had a sewing machine, I would sew right now!
2:40 PM-	Scratch that last thought. I cant use technology. Darn, I guess I could knit? But that would require learning. UGH
2:45 PM-	It has been a really long time since I spend time around the house. I usually get home and go straight into my room. Can you guess what I do? Yup, I get on the computer and my phone.

2:53 PM-   I swear I just heard my phone ring...... It's coming back to haunt me for not using it all day.

3:23 PM-   So me and [BoyFriend] drove to a friends house and knocked on the door to see if she wanted to hang out. At first she was really surprised to see us considering now a days you don't just show up to someones house. You call or text first. We didn't stay long because she was about to watch a movie. Darn

3:30 PM-   I think me and [BoyFriend] are going to start cleaning our room, but first I need to eat pronto before I have a fit.

3:54 PM-   I actually kind of like this, I feel like I am getting stuff done today.

3:58 PM-   Me and [BoyFriend] are seriously considering doing this whole "no digital" thing once a week.
Technology clouds our minds too much. Actually it is not technology all together, it is mostly just our phones that get in the way of what we need to get done.

4:21 PM-   Might I add, that I am MASTERING reading my watch, haha.

4:37 PM-   I have honestly never been so productive! I never noticed how much time I waste away on my phone daily! It is actually really sad. People should be able to go a whole day without their phone or any technology without freaking out. People make it too much of a necessity nowadays.

4:42 PM-   DANGIT, I walked back in my room and I was about to turn on some music. If I had a good voice I would sing instead, but I don't want to make [BoyFriend]s ears bleed.

5:10 PM-   This is the cleanest I HAVE EVER seen our room. Very nice.

5:19 PM-   Me and [BoyFriend] are going to build some roller coaster thingy. YAY!

5:42 PM-   I have kind of felt more hungry then usual today. I wonder if it is because my phone keeps me distracted more through out the day?

5:58 PM-   I wish we could at least turn on the radio. It seems so quiet. I haven't done anything like this since I was a child.

6:14 PM-   This is actually a lot of fun. I can't remember the last time me and [BoyFriend] actually hung out. We are usually sitting right next to each other, but we are both on our phones not saying a word to each other. This is nice.

6:36 PM-   I feel so happy actually having conversations with [BoyFriend] without being interrupted by a phone or being ignored because he is 'reading' something.
YAY FOR NO TECHNOLOGY.

7:20 PM-   If we had our phones this would never get finished or started. One of us would take a 'break' and get on our phone and just not come back to it. I just don't understand how cutting out one little thing can change the WHOLE course of your day.

8:05 PM-   I just noticed that the timing for today feels accurate. Usually my days go by so quick!
Every time I get on my phone I SPEND hours looking at crap, and before I know it the day is over and I did absolutely nothing. But today actually feel like a REAL day. Like when I used to be a little kid and the days were never ending!

8:32 PM-   We just finished building the roller coaster! It looks AWESOME! That was honestly so much fun. I definitely want to cut back on my cell phone usage. It makes me lazy. All I ever want to do is get on Facebook, Instagram, Ifunny, Pandora, and Youtube. I don't miss my phone that much right now. SWEEEEEET!

8:41 PM-   I'm going to take a shower. I'm not going to lie, I bet taking a shower without music on will SUCK even more than having no music during a car ride! It's going to be so boring. Ugh, Lame!

9:11 PM-   That shower wasn't as bad as I thought it would be. It would have been more relaxing with some music on, but that's okay. I don't HAVE to have it.

9:37 PM-   Me and [BoyFriend] just finished playing with our hamster. We don't know what to do anymore. I'm so tempted to watch a movie. DAMN YOU technology. We're probably going to walk around the house until we find something to do.

9:40 PM-   I'm going to play with my hair and try out some new styles, that is always fun! And I'm not being sarcastic. Haha

10:00 PM-   I am starving. I never thought I could get sick of Sandwiches, but I did. I really want some soup right now, but I have to use the microwave for that. SUCKS. Ooo some pizza sounds even better, but guess what? I CANT USE MY PHONE:(

10:16 PM-   So right about now is when I'm really wanting to use my phone. Every night before I go to bed I use it for how ever long it takes until I fall asleep. I'm really bored right now. I feel like me and [BoyFriend] have done everything there is to do. It was much funner having someone else do this with you.

10:39 PM-   I'm so ready for it to be 11PM so I can go to sleep! 20 more minutes. Oh, and I'm a pro at reading watches now. HECK YES!

10:47 PM-   I'm going to help [BoyFriend] make flash cards so he can study for one of his classes. I really wish I could catch up on some computer homework right now:(

11:00 PM-	This day has shown me that all the times I thought I didn't have time between work and school was CRAP! I have SO much time to get everything done on time with time to spare.
	I just waste my days away on my phone. I never thought that my phone was the problem. It hasn't even been a full 24 hours and by not using my phone throughout today I got more done than ever.
11:11 PM-	Well, I'm not tired anymore. Me and [BoyFriend] are probably going to keep studying for his course test. I kind of want to check my phone right now.
11:37 PM-	I am craving my phone right now. It is only when I get bored. See, It wouldn't be bad if I could stick to just checking my phone every once in awhile, but usually when I go to check it I get caught up looking at stuff and before I know it I have spent a couple hours just "checking" my phone. Technology now a days is definitely an addiction.
11:41 PM-	I'm going to paint my nails!
12:23 AM-	Okay well i'm probably going to bed now. Today was a wonderful life changing experience.
	That sounds silly considering all I did was just cut out technology for a day, but it really opened my eyes to a bad habit I didn't even know I had. Technology is a great thing, but at the same time it's horrible. It makes people lazy and dependent.

Conclusion: I am so happy I did this assignment. I think society is too caught up on everything being done digital, they do not want to do anything themselves because they can 'always' rely on technology. People are looking for ways to do less and less, before you know it they will invent a machine that walks for you so you don't have to anymore. Nobody knows what it is like to actually enjoy your days anymore without incorporating the stress of phones, social networks, and technology. This assignment definitely taught me a lot, I never knew how much I depended on my phone. Humans beings are supposed to interact with one another and be outside and active, not hide behind a text message and stay cooped up inside on the computer. This new generation needs a huge reality check. I wish everyone could do this assignment. You never know you have an addiction until you go a day with out it. My life will honestly never be the same after this. A lot of my day is spent on my phone, probably a good 5 or 6 hours a day. Wow. In that time I could get homework done, clean my room, clean my car, and spend time with my family. Everyone makes technology a necessity forgetting what it is like to live without it. If this is just the beginning, I wonder how society will be 30 years from now? It is very sad. Last but not least, Thank you Dr. G This assignment is probably the best thing that has come my way.

Delta.

-------------------------------------- **Report Ends Here** --------------------------------------

Note: This report is exactly as submitted, the only difference is I have changed the identifying data to protect the innocent. Other than that, this is my students exact report, bad grammar and all. This is an example of the level of detail, and the amount of thought that should be part of your experience and report as well. Enjoy!

24-hour Project

This is a second student's report. It, too, is outstanding. The content is unaltered from the original. Enjoy experiencing his day with him.

-------------------------------------- **Report 2 Starts Here** --------------------------------------

It's May 20, 2014, Tuesday, 11:00am, and I am just waking up to the alarm on my cell phone. I am checking all of my Facebook messages, texts, emails, voice mails, favorite apps, and using up my last few lives here on Candy Crush before I begin my 24-hour Project. I'm not the average student. I run my own business, being the go-to-guy for a lot of things, and I have a family, so I'm anxious and excited all at the same time; although, what's the point of living if everything was predictable, right? I know they normally recommend to begin at 8am however, if I did that then it wouldn't be as challenging for me; the majority of my digital activities are in the evening.

11:25 AM-	I am walking the house and checking my car, turning off all digital devices. I sure do hope I get them all.
11:30 AM-	Beginning the project.
11:48 AM-	Accidentally found a digital device that I forgot to shut off. I am turning my son's alarm clock face down. Normally, I never go in his room. This projects already starting to throw me off.
Noon	I am jumping in the shower and getting ready to go out and work.
12:18 PM-	I am fully dressed
12:29 PM-	I am sitting down on the couch contemplating how I am going to structure my day in the most efficient manner. I should of done planning yesterday. Luckily, I did at write down the contact information of my employees yesterday.
12:58 PM-	I decided to drive down the street to get a haircut. I have been trying to make the time to get it cut all last week, and I just never had the time. Now, I miraculously created time. Maybe I shoudn't play Pet Rescue so much.
1:20 PM-	I am craving some Chik Filet. I'm heading there now for brunch

1:40 PM-   It's time for me to begin working. Come to think about it, not using digital products shouldn't be hard (at least during the day) because I do have a manager that works for me that handles a lot of the problems if I am not around. I am having a blast! Not looking down at my phone every second makes life seem less stressful. It like a vacation actually. I say that now, but I think it will catch up to me later on.

1:48 PM-   My first inconvenience has just presented itself. I work in door to door sales selling security and home automation. I work with a crew of sales people and I forgot to call them last night to let them know where we will be meeting today. Well I didn't forget I was digitally preoccupied at the time. Ok I am here in Cedar Hill, Texas looking for an establishment that will allow me to use their phone to contact all my guys. I am pulling over here at a place called Ha-R-Charburgers. I looks homely enough. Surprisingly enough, they had an analog landline available for me to use. I did make contact with all the guys but one. I left a message and told him to call back at this number.

1:53 PM-   Owner kindly blurted out, "Mike, the telephone is for you." Wow, I haven't heard that one in a while.

1:55 PM-   I am sitting here in the booth at Hav-R-Charburgers just reflecting on how not using digital products could be a good thing in this day and age, especially in business. I mean not using my cell phone was an inconvenience: I had to go out of my way 20-30 minutes making the necessary calls that could have otherwise been avoided by a simple group text. Sigh.

2:00 PM-   It just hit me! I've always been bad at scheduling and preparing. Had I sacrificed 30 mins of Pet Rescue last night, I wouldn't of had to do it today. I've always found it challenging to schedule and prepare for things because it just feels like I don't have time to; attempting to remember to do it later seems more preferably at the time. Lesson learned: less time on time consuming digital devices creates more time to prepare for the next day. Hey! I did learn that I Hav-R-Charburgers is friendly enough to let me stand at their counter and make consecutive calls.

2:25 PM-   I found a 35 cent payphone. Hey didn't it used to be 25 cents to place a call? I mean they even had a saying, "here is a quarter, call somebody who cares."

2:50 PM-   I have been having an enlightening discussion about the Sabbath with one of my guys while we wait for everyone to show up. Dialog is great! Debating is even better. Normally, we would be face down engulfed in our own digital distractions.

3:00 PM-   I am starting my training session. We do not use any digital products during this portion of my job to the next couple of hours should be a cinch.

5:07 PM-   It's time to head home.

5:15 PM-   A song popped into my head, making me wish I could turn on Satellite Radio, Ch 8, 80's

5:32 PM-   Traffic!! Ok now I am really wishing I could get on to my device. I hate sitting in traffic with nothing to do. Normally, I check my messages or look for back roads to take.

5:50 PM-   Finally, made it passed all that construction/traffic!

5:57 PM-   I am walking into the house.

6:05 PM-   I'm engaged in a conversation with my son. We do not talk much. Normally, I am on my phone and he is on his video game itouch device. I am a little emotional right now; he just told me about a near death experience that he was involved in, that I was unaware of. An experience that happened over 5 years ago. And- how did this conversation just now come up? Is it coincidental that it's surfacing at the same time that I'm coming up for air out of the digital lagoon. Wow. I need to invest more time in my parenting. I love my kids but it's just so hard to with work and trying to start a new business.

6:35 PM-   ] I am going to detail the van. So, I bought this van 3 weeks ago from the auction and have been so busy that I have not had the time to clean it or even post an ad for it. That 3 weeks that I've been sitting on my investment. Today that all changes.

6:50 PM-   I am taking a break to journal here. While I was scrubbing the dirt out of the carpets, I was thinking about the effectiveness and purpose of this project. I was calculating in my head how many minutes I waste playing the 5 lives you are given in Candy Crush; it came to about 30 minutes. Then I added in how many minutes I spent on Facebook scrolling the news feed while waiting for new lives to generate (it takes 30 minutes to generate 1 life.) I spend usually 45 minutes on Facebook in the news feed. Then I wasted another 15 minutes playing the lives that generated while I was on Facebook. That is a grand total of 90 minutes (an hour and a half.) This occurs multiple times a day, every day of the week. All this time, I've been trying to find time to clean the van and list it for sale. I'm shaking my head (SMH) because it's been in front of me this whole time. All I can say is, "wow."

7:42 PM-   I am filthy. I just finished cleaning the van and am drenched with dirt and sweat. I am jumping directly in the shower now; not passing go, not collecting $200.

8:06 PM-   I decided to do something different. My blood is still flowing from the cleaning the van. I'm going to cook to night. Now although I love to cook, this is not routine in our home. Normally, we eat out; I'm the only cook in the house and I frequently spend my most of my time loafing on the couch googling things to Google or sending meaningless tweets to people. Understand, I am the "Italian Stallion" and I am a maniacal chef. I make a mean Shrimp Scampi that will make you slap your mama. Oh my gosh (OMG) I really didn't remember how bad I needed new cookware.

8:49 PM-   We are all sitting at the table eating tonight. Kodak moment!! This just doesn't happen around here. When you get your food from a drive through or Togo from a restaurant, it's paper and plastic and therefore we eat in the living room in front of the TV. However, this chef's Italian cuisine calls for breaking out the fine china and sterling silverware. We are actually conversing at the dinner table. Who are these people laugh out loud (lol.)

9:42 PM-   Since I'm the one on the digital diet, I elected to be the designated dishwasher; everyone else is in the other room watching my favorite shows. Actually, I don't mind. I have this rare condition of OCD that only presents itself after I begin projects. I am more thorough when it comes to washing dishes than anyone I know. I scrub the insides and outsides of all the glasses and bowls and scrub all ends of the silverware instead of letting the dish washing machine do it. Everyone else always leaves that occasional trace of lipstick or that one dish with a spec of food on it, but not I.

10:12 PM-   The hardest hours are upon me as the rest of my family begins to wind down for bed, I'm normally up late surfing the web, watching Netflix, watching Hulu, texting, playing back to back games and listening to music.

10:30 PM-   First thing on the list is exercise.

10:35 PM-   "Darn it! No Ipod." I do have a portable CD player, but that will skip since I can't set it up on the treadmill. Why can't I set it up on a treadmill?? Because it's digital!

10:40 PM-   I am all suited up, limber and beginning my 4 mile jog to military cadence. Oh what sweet memories.

11:49 PM-	What a workout! I'm extremely overheated right now. Wow, I should of worked my way up to that workout. I really missed having my music; it takes my mind off of the pain. However, I did enjoy sounding off some Marine Corps cadence. I really need some water right now. Clearly, I am out of shape. Tomorrow- I always say tomorrow I'm going to start my workout. Tomorrow I'm going to begin my diet. I am really glad that I committed to doing this "digital diet." I think I've finally ended my procrastination when it comes to working out. Day 1 started TODAY.
12:04 PM-	I just finished taking my 3rd shower of the day. I'm loving the 3 a day showers.
12:12 PM-	I am going to drive to the local 7-11 to grab a large Gatorade.
12:28 AM-	It is extremely boring right now. This is prime time for Face-booking amongst my friends. Ugh! I know by 2:30am everyone will be asleep and I won't have anyone to chat with. Oh wait. I did tell everyone that I was going to be on by 2:30am. They probably waiting up to hear how the 24-hour project went. I hope so.
12:32 AM-	Tic Toc, Tic Toc.
12:40 AM-	I am rereading Chapter 6 in my CMPTR 2 book. I really enjoyed the section on privacy. I actually quite disappointed that we flew so quickly through the chapter with it being such a relevant topic in today's times. While I was waiting in line at the 7-11 tonight, I read a headline in the newspaper (dated 5/20/2014) that the U.S. is charging five military officers of the Chinese army for cyber crimes involving the theft of trade secrets from U.S. Steel Westinghouse Electric Co. We may not have a country left to do power points for, databases for, and workbooks for if these invasions persist. I'm just saying...if privacy issues make national headlines, maybe we should talk a little more about it.
12:50 AM-	It's hard to concentrate with my son's cell phone pinging with Instagram notifications and FB messages. I can hear it all the way in the living room. Wait! My house. My rules.
12:51 AM-	Ping = Gone
1:50 AM-	I read the whole Security and Privacy section of Chapter 6. Wow I got so much more out of it the second time.
2:00 AM-	I really enjoyed this project, not just because I didn't use digital devices but because I never really journaled before. Inspirational speakers and life coaches preach to do it, but I never really had the time to do it so wrote it off as impossible for me and my lifestyle. I can't wait to reread this stuff.

2:08 AM-   I am eating celery and peanut butter. Negative calories meets all natural protein. It's the only way to go.

2:22 AM-   The tension is heightening. I don't know if I am more excited about checking my phone or writing my conclusion.

2:24 AM-   I am going to spend the last 6 minutes on my conclusion.

Conclusion: The 24-hour project has forever changed my mentality in regards to how I allow digital devices to rule my life. Instead of living to go digital, I will go digital only to live. You might think I'm crazy, but having the conversation today with my son and giving him my full attention proved to negate the need of our over-priced psychologist. Our problems seemed to make tremendous headway with undivided attention alone. Facetiously, I remember several sessions where I would be glancing at my cell phone and sending a short text message here and there, and the psychologist never said anything to me for doing so or mentioning to in private how it could have an effect on the family. Perhaps it was because I was cutting the checks. Come to think of it, why was I paying him again?? Now I am not trying to escape digital all together. It provides great benefits. If anything, I will sacrifice some of the time on my digital devices from here moving forward and use the time saved to salvage what relationship I have left with my son and hopefully repair what was lost. This 24 hour undertaking (if you can't tell) has had an astounding affect on me and my life (<3 this project.) Additionally, my wife and I divorced back in 2010. She said that I never helped around the house, nor did I spend any quality time with her anymore. Until now, I thought she was crazy. I really felt I was the same guy she met when we dated, if not better. Yeah I am working more, but for her and the family! This 24 hour activity (because of it's nature) has my mind spinning back in time, stimulating my reflection process and wondering what could have become of my life had I done this simple underrated project sooner. I have to admit, she was right. I literally had an affair with my cell phone. I remember one time we were on a date, I was doing a lot of business on my phone that night. At the time I didn't realize it, but she was engaged in a 5 minute side-bar conversation with our waiter because he was waiting on me to order. I was too busy on the phone making a deal happen. Funny thing is I am not even with that company anymore. Combined, there were hundreds of thousands of cell minutes, texts, tweets, emails and surfs that I allowed to come before her. Talk about regrets. I lost someone that I loved and more importantly, someone who loved me more than I could even love myself, and that could have been avoided had I just made time for her. Throughout these adventurous 1,440 minutes, the absence of digital has revealed we have all the time in the world resting in the palms of our hands. "Geez! I cant believe how we get so consumed without even realizing it! Live Laugh Love before it's too late"

Also, I have to admit, this venture was like a blueprint to efficiency; it helped me discover how much time I had to get things done. I knocked out several tasks that I had been procrastinating on like cleaning my van and getting my hair cut. I literally felt like I could stop and smell the roses throughout the entire day with all "looking down" every 5 minutes to see if I had a missed call or text. Ironically, I didn't really crave my digital gadgets as badly as I thought I would. Perhaps my subconsciousness too was long overdue for an analog retreat. I wouldn't doubt it. I traditionally use over 5,000 minutes mobile minutes and rack up over 5 gigs of data usage per month on my cell phone.

In closing, I believe that by doing this project, it may have been the only wedge in my digital life that allowed me to see that I am truly an addict, digital is a drug, and I've been overdosing to the point that the "digital high" was killing my offline reality. Dr. G. thanks for suggesting I do this 24-hour project. Thanks for staying on me: continuously encouraging me to get it done; it made a difference. I seriously hope that through my gain, you would keep recommending it to everyone. You never know whose future you could be saving next semester because of your unorthodox ideas like this 24 hour experiement.

It's now 2:51am. I went 21 minutes over. Yay!

CPSIA information can be obtained
at www.ICGtesting.com
Printed in the USA
LVHW020815040119
602719LV00004B/28/P